Unbreakable Cord

by

Karen Barquero

DORRANCE
PUBLISHING CO
EST. 1920
PITTSBURGH, PENNSYLVANIA 15238

Dorrance Publishing Co
585 Alpha Drive
Pittsburgh, PA 15238
Visit our website at www.dorrancebookstore.com

ISBN: 979-8-89027-087-0
eISBN: 979-8-89027-585-1

INTRODUCTION

"A method to my madness." This is the phrase that I believe best describes my approach to sobriety. Before I go any further, I want to set the stage. I am in prison, serving thirteen years. I am an addict, and there are drugs all around me twenty-four seven. I am currently fourteen months sober.

What was the method? Madness. I realized something very profound during my quest for sobriety. No two people are the same. It sounds elementary. And it is, if you only remain on the surface. Addiction and our various pathways leading up to it are all unique. Millions of roads leading to the same destination. And if you are to unravel the steps you took to get where you are, a standardized method is not what you need. Madness. You must be willing to approach the madness with an open and willing mind.

This method of madness I have discovered is almost tailormade for the type of environment I found sobriety in. A mad house. A place where you can't escape temptation. There is no locking your door and shutting the world out. There is no clean and drug-free environment to run to. This is guerilla warfare. You are in the trenches, day in and day out. As soon as you decide that you want to stop using, someone is in your face with an abundance of your favorite drug. In this sort of setting there is only one way to truly attack your addiction. And that is at the root of the problem.

Welcome to my method of madness.

CHAPTER 1
NEXT TIME

It was once said that addiction can be likened to a steel cable. Each strand that's weaved into the cable makes it stronger and stronger, until at last you cannot break it....

Drugs are fun. Until they're not. This will not be your run-of-the-mill book on recovery. This book was written from my very own life experiences. And though you and I may have different stories, we share the same problem: addiction.

This work takes an honest and hard look at the deepest laid roots of addiction. As we touch on the different issues which plague us as addicts, do not expect to be coddled or handled gently. You will receive nothing but the cold hard truth of the matter at hand: your addiction.

It is completely up to you, the reader, my fellow sister or brother in the struggle, to make the change. There is no magic wand to be waved, or a particular set of words to be said that will free you of the chains of addiction. The responsibility rests fully on you. Sucks, I know. But it's something you have to want and crave, just as, if not more than, the drug itself.

I am not some "expert" who spent his youth doing all of the right things and graduating from some prestigious university with an inflated idea of what it means to be an addict. No disrespect to those individuals; if the world had more people like them, there would be less addicts like me.

With that being said, I am you, the addict. I'm the person who has tried every drug, and found an extreme liking to a few. I've robbed, stolen, lied, cheated, and so much more, all for the sake of drugs. I'm the person who started getting high with friends at the tender age of twelve, and ended up spending the next twenty years on an uncontrollable rollercoaster of outstanding highs and terrifying lows. All because "it's what all the cool kids are doing," or at least that's how the story started....

Summer 1999, last day of the eighth-grade year. Jacksonville, FL.

I remember scrambling around, trying to find out what everyone was going to be doing that day. It was, after all, the last time we would ever be middle schoolers again. Next stop, high school. As I ran into a group of kids who, when looking back, did everything in their power to ditch me at every turn were sneaking off school grounds two class periods early, I, of course, had to join them.

"Do you smoke pot?" they asked me.

"Hell yeah I do," knowing I was lying. But we were already a mile down the road. And the whole way there Tess and I were making those adolescently flirtatious eyes at each other. I couldn't turn back now.

"You got any money? We're about to meet with our dealer," she asked me.

I did have money. My mom had given it to me so that me and my best friend Dustin could go to the mall. Shit, Dustin. I had completely forgotten about him. Hopefully I can make it back in time for when school lets out. Little did I know that this day would not only go nothing how I planned it, but it would set in motion a lifetime of bad choices, where I'd continually let down all the right people in order to please all of the wrong ones.

"Yeah, I've got twenty bucks," I said, thinking that it had the ring of a thousand.

Tess smiled and held her hand out. I gladly gave her the twenty-dollar bill without so much as a second thought. I was the definition of "a sucker for a big butt and smile." Once she had gotten the money from me, all of the special attention she had been showing me was suddenly gone. The smile, the twinkle in her eye, it all vanished.

"Wait here," the blond kid said; this was the first thing he'd said to me the whole way. I remember wanting to impress him the most out of the bunch. And he was the one who seemed to like me the least. It was this kid, the cool and popular guy that had all the friends and all the girls, who I don't even remember his name, that I looked up to and wanted to be like.

He turned and left; they all followed him. "Wait here?"

"Why? Where are y'all going?" I asked. Tess turned with annoyance in her face and voice.

"We told you, going to meet our dealer. He don't like new faces. Just wait here. We'll be right back. Two minutes tops." She ran back and gave me a small kiss on the cheek. And with that, the deal was sealed. I was sold.

They disappeared between two houses, jumping a fence and heading into the ditch that ran behind them through the neighborhood. I stood there for nearly thirty minutes before reality sunk in. That was the last time I saw Tess that summer.

Walking home from an area I wasn't all that familiar with, I cursed those stupid kids every step of the way. I vowed all sorts of revenge should I ever run into them again. It was all the blond kid's fault. He didn't want me to steal his shine and take his spotlight.

But that was just a lie I told myself, trying to avoid the truth of it. It was me who had given them my money. I was the one who put my trust in the wrong people. I told myself that something like that would never happen again. That I would never again do something so stupid. That I would never again put my trust in someone. Never ever again. Instead, NEXT TIME, I would be the one to get over.

As a person who was once subject to his addiction, I can accurately say that we, as a whole, have many falsely attuned and applied concepts by which we live our lives. Concepts that, when used in a positive manner, would have done us wonders in the way of success. And the concept I'd like to bring attention to here is called NEXT TIME.

So, continuing on, in the beginning, I had no idea that this NEXT TIME mentality would become one of the greatest hindrances on my life. That it would go on to affect all of my choices and greatly distort my view of nearly every event in my life.

The NEXT TIME mentality began to create a vacuum in my life which would never allow me to cut my losses and simply walk away. Rather, it would lead me to continually chase the proverbial dream, as they say. A chase that if never abandoned, can only end one of two ways.

When we operate in the NEXT TIME mindset, what we're doing, essentially, is building a habit of always expecting a win. We take away our ability to "learn from the situation," because all we can see is the potential for a win, NEXT TIME, and in the place of learning, comes "yearning."

We yearn for the opportunity to approach the same exact situation with the hopes of possibly conquering it NEXT TIME. By definition, that would be called determination. And determination is a good thing. Determination is what separates success from failure. This is all true. With the exception of one small detail: the drug.

Example: This person got my money and never brought my drugs back. A rookie move, as we would call it. The broken perception of how to handle the situation in the future would look something like this: "NEXT TIME, I'll get the product first," or, "NEXT TIME, I won't let the money out of my sight." It's obvious that the most logical way of dealing with that issue is to cut your losses and move on to something else.

If I go to Tony's Cafe and find a roach in my spaghetti, or you paid for delivery that you never received, I'd be a fool to go back and try Tony's Cafe again. NEXT TIME I'll just order the lasagna, or I'll just go inside and order. In this instance, Tony's Cafe is the Drug. As addicts, we don't realize that Tony's Cafe, or, rather, the Drug, is the problem. It's not the type of drug, or the amount of drug, or the form of payment. No, it's the drug.

Let me paint it this way. If you get caught in a burning building and you lose all of your stuff, but you make it out alive, will you go to another burning building to try it again with hopes that this time you might come out of it with all or some of the stuff? Absolutely not. Any yet and still, the addict will return to the drug time after time, in hopes of conquering it; even after losing everything, we still come back to the drug. We don't learn. We yearn.

This concept directly affects the addict for one very simple reason: Every time we do drugs, we lose. No matter how you try to rationalize it. We take a loss each and every time we get high. Whether it be financially, socially, or physically. When you use drugs, you take a proverbial step backwards in life. It may be a big step, or a small step, but backwards, nonetheless. And backwards is not forwards. Nothing can be gained from getting high. Trust me, I've tried.

We spend valuable money, whether hard earned or easily acquired, on a thing which will be gone in a few hours or even worse, a few minutes. Sure, you may have enjoyed it while it lasted, but once it's gone, you're right back where you started. Nothing was gained.

You may be saying to yourself, "What's the difference between spending my money on a drug I enjoy and spending my money on a movie or theme park I enjoy?" I know, because this used to be my reasoning as well.

A theme park won't land you in prison. A movie can't kill you. And neither one of those can become an insatiable habit that will control your every decision. That's not all, I can also hear all of those other excuses you've formed to try and reason away how doing drugs are harmful. It plays in my head just like it plays in yours. "What about people that have good-paying jobs and can enjoy some recreational cocaine on the weekends?" or "What about the person who rides around all day selling drugs and doing them. They're making money, they're doing fine."

Are they? What happens when the person with a good job gets busted coming from their dealer? Or what if their kids pick up the habit? Or if the drug use spills over into Monday morning and it begins to affect their performance at work? No more good job, no more happy home. How many stresses and concerns does the drug dealer have to withstand on a continual basis? Will I get robbed? Will the cops stop me? Will someone rat me out?

The ROOTS of all of our problems are the issues we have discussed in this chapter and will discuss in the chapters to come. The drug is the TREE that grows from those ROOTS. The addiction is nothing more than the BRANCHES that grow from the drug TREE. Getting taken for your money or buying a bad batch or getting busted are all just FRUITS on the BRANCHES of addiction.

It's imperative that we stop trying to simply pluck the fruit off, trim the branches, or even cut down the tree. Because fruit bears in its season, and branches grow back even from a stump of a cut down tree. We must dig it up from the ROOT; this way, NEXT TIME, there won't be a NEXT TIME.

CHAPTER 2
ISOLATION

Growing up, my family was a tight-knit group. Aunts, uncles, cousins, grandparents, and, of course, the immediate family, Mom, Dad, and sis. We looked like the family from *Home Alone*, dysfunctional but loving. Every holiday, birthday, and most weekends, we would get together to enjoy each other's company. Sometimes it would be a pool party or a backyard BBQ. Sometimes we'd go out to the movies or a water park. And other times we'd go on camping trips. But we were always together.

It would seem as though this sort of family-oriented upbringing would be ideal to a kid's development. And it is, until drugs get thrown into the mix.

This was a very foundational time in my addiction. The steel cord I was weaving had gone into an accelerated process, and strand after strand was being laid several times a day.

I must give you a quick disclaimer before I continue with this part of the story. I no longer blame others for my actions. I used to, but now for me to say that another person is the cause of my actions is to say that I'm nothing more than a robot, controlled by others, subject to another person's will. A slave. And that, I am not. I am fully responsible for every decision I've ever made.

So now that we have gotten that out of the way, let's continue. My cousins and I were best of friends. We were smoking buddies. Whenever we'd get together, pot, pills, and drinking were at the center of it. And these family functions were the perfect opportunity to meet up and do our drugs. Plus, what better way to enjoy a BBQ or a water park or camping than to be high. Right?

Wrong. That is the mindset of an addict. The drug tells you that "you will not have fun unless you use me." So as the months and years went on, and with each family gathering, in my mind, it became more and more, about me and my cousins getting high than actually enjoying the company of loved ones. The very concept of family had become synonymous with drugs. This was life threatening and terminally detrimental to each and every one of the relationships I would ever have for the rest of my drug-involved life.

The time came when my family started to become aware of my drug use. Once this happened, they were harder on me and paid more attention whenever we would have our family functions. It came to a point that I could no longer use drugs while at these functions, so what did I do? I stopped going.

I began to choose the drug, which had no feelings and ultimately would destroy my life, over the people who did have feelings. Over the people who did have my best interest at heart. Plain and simple, I chose drugs over my family. And soon enough, I began to arrive at the point where I was harboring feelings of resentment and anger because the "family stuff" was getting in the way of my "getting high stuff." With that came my decision to opt out of family functions altogether.

This strand of my addiction cord became entirely too toxic. I had just successfully ISOLATED myself from anyone or anything that could have helped me with my addiction. If you think that this occurred by chance, or that it was not done by design, you are sadly mistaken.

In the wild, when a lion or a pack of hyenas are on the hunt, the first thing they do is locate their target. They go over all the available options and try to find the most vulnerable out of them all. This usually ends up being the runt or the youngest of the herd they are hunting. Once the target has been selected, the next step for the skilled predators is to remove and ISOLATE the target. This ISOLATION rips us of any security we might have. It desecrates our defenses. And commandeers our security.

As human beings, we were not created to be alone. No creature was. Read what it says in Genesis 2:18: "...It is not good that man should be alone."

God said that. Then watch what happens next in that same story. Satan comes along and finds Adam's wife all alone, whispers some words of doubt in her ear, and the rest is history. This is why ISOLATION is so dangerous and leaves us so susceptible to attack. When the natural order of things is out of whack, especially regarding our innate need to belong, a sense of confusion tends to settle in its place. Confusion as to who we are and what our purpose is.

Drugs are a tool used by the enemy in order to ISOLATE us. Who's the enemy, you ask? Satan. And in his best efforts to destroy your life he must first ISOLATE you from all the things which are good for you in your life. He wants you to be placed on an uncharted island in the middle of nowhere, where you will be left to fend for yourself. All alone.

Some of you may be saying, "Well, I never had a family. So this doesn't apply to me." Maybe you didn't have a family when you were growing up. Or maybe you did, but there wasn't a very strong bond between you. One thing I can assure you is that there was something or someone in your life who was GOOD for you, and had your best interest in mind. Perhaps a spouse or lover, or maybe a schoolteacher or counselor at school, or a job, or an employee at the job. If you pushed that person away, the one thing which was GOOD for you in your life, if you pushed it away in exchange for the drug, then this most definitely applies to you.

Once you are alone, the enemy swoops in and makes its move. It comes in the form of addiction. The addiction itself is what the enemy uses to try and give you a false sense of security. It's not that we don't know we're addicted, we just don't realize what that actually means.

In the early stages of our addictions, we are led to believe that the addiction is the thing in which we can find solace. We don't need anyone. Just give us our drug. If you have ever pushed someone good away and said in your mind that you don't need them, rest assured that the enemy was hard at work. In essence what you have done was taken your natural-born NEED for human connection and traded it for the synthetic NEED of a drug.

It's evil in every sense of the word. We are tricked and manipulated into thinking that the addiction, the insatiable appetite we have for drugs, is actually good for us. We find comfort in knowing that should we withstand an attack, it will be there for us as a shield. We get pulled into a trusting relationship with our addiction. We end up resting in the reassurance of its consistency. And ultimately, we come to know that it will never leave us. What we don't know is that it never leaving us IS the ATTACK.

The thing I came to learn from this is that a relationship is easier to destroy than it is to repair. I only know this because I've finally come to the point in my recovery where I can clearly see just how important my relationships with others are.

But this is not about me or my progress in recovery. It's about you and your progress. Facing the reality that we have seriously damaged a person's emotions, self-confidence, and even love for us, all for the sake of doing drugs, is a very tough pill to swallow. (Pun intended.) It's an ugly truth that we try and avoid. A truth that we will do everything in our power not to look at. But look at it, you must.

I'm here to tell you that until you begin to make steps towards repairing those broken relationships, you will never see any results. It'll be one of your greatest moments of healing yet....

If you're like me and have no clue on where to start with a thing like this, try this exercise out and see if it works for you.... Look in a mirror. Imagine that the person you are staring at is the same one you've pushed away. Put yourself in their shoes. Recall all of the times you've mistreated them. Think back to every time you've left them hanging. Every time you've lied to them. Imagine all the things that they'd like to say to you. Every pain-induced truthful word that they may have been harboring, waiting for the day to unload them on you and cut you to the core. And say them out loud.

Do this, and just know that the way you feel is only but a small portion of the way they actually feel. Now here's the hard part. Oh yes, that was only the beginning, my friend. Remember nothing worth having comes easy. So again, here's the hard part: go to that person, and apologize. Apologize from the deepest depths of your heart. Ask them if they would allow you to come back in their life.

Remember, we were made to have relationships. It's in our God-given nature to want to maintain companionship. Reconcile those relationships and watch as the life-changing healing begins to take place.

CHAPTER 3
EXCUSE vs. REASON

June 2013

I had just been released after doing four years in an Arkansas prison and was now ready to get on with my life. I had all sorts of plans and hopes for my future. Some were positive, but most were not.

"Man, I really want to smoke some weed, but I'm going to have to take a piss test in a few days for my PO," I told my cousin.

"I don't know why they don't just let you guys get high. This stuff ain't that bad," he said.

"Right, if I would be allowed to smoke weed then I wouldn't do other drugs."

"I got a way you can smoke and still pass that test. It's a drink to clean your system out. It'll make you piss clean, one hundred percent of the time," he said.

"You can get it?"

"Right from the store. Twenty bucks and you're good to go."

That was all I needed. A way out was provided, and I jumped on board. I can smoke pot and not get in trouble for it. I was in search for an Excuse to start getting high again and I found one. But was it the Reason?

EXCUSE vs. REASON

I want to draw attention to an issue that plagues many addicts. Our excuses.

We form excuses and do it with the misconception that what we came up with was a reason. So let's see what the definition is for EXCUSE: a reason, real or pretended.

In order to gain a full and proper perspective on the matter the next thing we must do is find out what is the definition for REASON: Draw conclusions or inferences from facts or premises. Right thinking.

So, an excuse is a reason that may or may not be right or has factual backing. Whereas a reason is right. A reason is backed by facts. A Reason is the TRUTH.

Let's be honest with ourselves for a moment. How many times have we made excuses for the things we do in comparison to having found a reason for doing them? Note that you make an Excuse, but Find a Reason. If I "find" the keys to my car, then I know where they are, and my car will start. They become a fact. They become Truth. But if I "make" a set of keys for my car, then they may or may not work; my car might not start. They are not a fact. They are not truth. That's the difference between making Excuses and finding the Reason.

Here are some examples of excuses and reasons:

Excuse: "I do drugs because they make me feel good."

Reason: "I do drugs because I don't know what else to turn to to try and ease my discomfort, pain, and anxiety. And when I get high it makes me forget all of my shortcomings and insecurities."

Excuse: "I do drugs because they spark my creativity."

Reason: "I do drugs because when I'm not high I can't focus on anything other than getting high, and me not being able to focus will block my creativity."

Excuse: "I do drugs because it's my choice. I can do what I want."

Reason: "I do drugs because I have a lack of control in my life and am trying to find a way to exercise my freedom to make my own decisions, and I won't let anyone tell me any different."

Can you see how an excuse will conveniently leave out certain aspects of the truth in order to make it easier to accept? Excuses are manufactured using our own perception of what's acceptable in society. Excuses are crafted out of a need to impress or win someone over. Excuses are nothing more than a quilt weaved together with threads of insecurities and a lack of self-confidence. And we use that quilt to cover ourselves and to hide from reality.

But Reasons, those are something different altogether. Reasons are what we find in the reality of a situation, regardless of how acceptable it may or may not be. Reason comes with a requirement of courage. We have to be courageous enough to step out from the status quo, to separate ourselves from the crowd and make a stand against what the masses are doing or agreeing with. Reason holds a mirror up to our ugliness, to our faults, to our weaknesses. When we finally decide to start looking at our Reason for doing things and not the Excuse, only then can we expect to see clearly the honest and true picture of who we are.

If you go back and examine those examples of excuse and reason you will find a key phrase within them: "Because I can."

BECAUSE I CAN

How many of us in this world want nothing more than to maintain full and complete control of our lives? Nearly everyone.

Many times in our lives, we do things for no other reason than to simply exercise our sovereign right to make our own decision. Hence, when we use drugs. I do them because it's my body, it's my life, and I'll do as I please.

While this is true—it is your body, it is your life, and you can do as you please—is doing drugs really the way to exercise that? Let's be honest, when we do drugs, who are we benefiting? It's most definitely not ourselves. The drug dealer for one. I can't tell you how many days in a row I've handed over six to seven hundred dollars, and still wasn't satisfied. The drug I received was gone that night and those six hundred bucks, a week's salary for most Americans, can never be reimbursed. It would have been no different if I were to have set the cash on fire and used the flames to warm my hands. And I've done this daily, for MONTHS!

But this goes deeper than how much money your addiction has cost you. The need to assert ourselves in regard to the amount of willpower, or the level of control we have over our decisions, is something that everyone experiences. And the addict suffers greatly from this.

By taking a drug, you may be under the impression that you are exercising your freedom of choice. But let's examine what true willpower looks like.

Someone yells at you and calls you every name in the book except the son of God. True willpower is to ignore that person. However, we give in to the desire of the attacking person when we respond in the same aggressive manner. A confrontation is obviously what that person wants. And by giving in and responding, you would be doing what they want, not what you want.

If your neighbor's spouse entices you to sleep with them while their other half is at work, your first impulse is to indulge in the desire. But don't give in! To do so would be to violate all the trust your neighbor has placed in you.

If I lead you to the world's tallest cliff and present the option for you to jump to your death, would you do it? Why not? You would be exercising the express dominion over your life and the freedom to do as you please. Of course you wouldn't jump, it's just not logical. (If you would then this book is not for you. Please seek help by calling the suicide hotline.) You always have the option not to jump. You always have the right to choose not to give in to what I want you to do.

Pay close attention here. When you refrain from doing a thing, when you choose not to do something, that's when you exercise your will to its fullest strength. Giving in to what the enemy would have you do is pure weakness. Why do you think the Ten Commandments given by God are filled with "thou shall not..." When we go against what is easy and what feels good in the moment, that's true willpower.

God created us to be champions. And unless you go through a battle you will never know what victory is. How can you win if you don't compete? So, compete against those whimsical desires, compete against every random urge that will do nothing more than set you back in life. Start exercising YOUR will and stop giving in to the enemies.

Chapter 4

DO I KNOW YOU?

I once took on the task of writing anonymous letters to guys who are on twenty-three-hour-a-day lockdown. Guys who are only allowed out of their rooms for one hour of rec (a caged in area outside that's the same size of their room) and for a shower. And as I wrote the first word on that page, a question came to mind....

DO I KNOW YOU?

The answer should be obvious. I'm writing an anonymous letter to someone I've never met. So, no, I do not know this person. Right...?

Wrong. Several other questions came to me directly after:

*Has this person ever experienced pain?

*Has this person ever felt the sting of being insulted?

*Has this person ever felt betrayed?

*If this person were to make a wish list, would freedom and happiness be somewhere near the top of it?

*Embarrassed?

*Lonely?

*What about love? Do they need love?

The answer to all of those would be yes. Each and every one of us has endured the same things. Granted, the circumstances and degree of those things vary. But the truth remains the same, we have all experienced each and every one of those things.

And with that understanding I realized that though I may not be able to look you in the face and call your name out. And though I may not ever even meet you physically. I may not know all of the details of your life, or how a certain chapter or event may have affected you. I still know you. I can still relate to the effects in your life. I know you spiritually.

So as you read about the next chapter of my life, keep in mind that although the details may be different, the basis is still the same....

OCTOBER 2014

I met a girl who lived down the street from me. At this time I had been out of prison from my first bid for over a year. Smoking weed and snorting coke had once again become part of my life. And the relationship I formed with this girl was based solely on two things. The first was sex. And looking back, I was under the impression that this was the main component of our relationship. I was wrong; the glue which held us together was the drug.

After being together for only one month, she introduced me to a drug called Roxy. It's a synthesized form of heroin, prescribed to people with pain problems. A pain pill. I smile every time I hear that phrase now. Not because it brings me joy, but because of the play on words. A pill that's supposed to take your pain away does just the opposite; it creates pain. A pain pill. (I'll get more into that in a later chapter.)

This newly explored drug festered an addiction inside of me unlike any I had ever known. It didn't take years to settle in and become a habit. It didn't start off in a party atmosphere disguised as a friendly past time. There was no gentleness to it, no subtlety. It came in hard, and it came in fast, like a jet crash landing on a city street. It had zero concern for my wellbeing or for the wellbeing of anyone around me.

Our current living conditions, i.e., our parents, were a big hindrance to us doing our drug in peace. So, after just two short months of knowing each other, we decided to move in together. And the nearest and cheapest hotel was the place we decided to live. A real hole-in-the-wall roach motel. A place where cops had to install a substation at, just because of all of the crime, murders, and overdoses that occurred there.

At other times when we didn't have enough money for a room, we would park the car somewhere hidden and sleep in the car. We would tell each other that living like this was all because of our love for one another. That we'd sacrifice anything for each other. But that was only a lie; we did it because of our love for the drug. The relationship was nothing more than a covering to help us hide from the reality of our addiction. Think about it. If we were willing to sacrifice anything, why not the drug, so we could afford a place to live?

My addiction to pain pills got so bad that within two months of me being introduced to them, I quit my job. A very good job, that paid me over eight hundred dollars a week. The pills that I was addicted to, they cost me thirty bucks a piece. Yes, a thirty-dollar pill. And between the two of us, we were doing no less than ten to fifteen a day. That's, at the very minimum, three hundred dollars a day and $2,100 a week. Keep in mind I was still smoking weed and doing coke and molly, in addition to my twelve pack of beer I drank daily and her pack of cigarettes she smoked daily. Factor in the cost of our room along with food and gas in the car. Our total weekly cost of living was well into the four-thousand-dollar range.

This is where the drug held no concern for my wellbeing. This is where the desperation of trying to maintain my addiction brought me to an all-time low, and my life took its turn for the worst.

Stealing became my job. All day long. I would drop her off at work and ride around all day, scouting the sides of houses and stores for tools or merchandise left unattended. Once I had a couple hundred bucks worth, I'd pull into a pawn shop, cash in, and already be calling up my dealer before I got back into the car. But even that wasn't enough. I would print my own ten-dollar bills and change them out at fast food drive-thrus, asking the cashier, once the register was opened, to trade me as many big bills as they could stand. I'd pull away from the window with at least a hundred bucks.

There's a verse in the Bible from Ecclesiastes 1:7–8 that says, "All the rivers run into the sea. Yet the sea is not full. To the place from which the rivers run, there they return again. All things are full of labor man cannot express it. THE EYE IS NOT SATISFIED WITH SEEING, NOR THE EAR FILLED WITH HEARING."

The truth of that verse was about to be brought to fullness in my life. Because on top of those two illegal means of gaining money, a third was taken on. This particular business venture involved my girlfriend whom I held at night, and kissed in the morning, the woman whom I professed to have loved. I was held by such a tight grip of an addiction that I agreed to help her in doing something completely contrary to what love is.

She would leave her day job and start her night job. We spent our evenings driving from house to house from hotel to hotel, selling herself.

That's not love. That's confusion. We had no idea who we were. We were willing, as a pair, to succumb to our lowest lows. To completely degrade and demean ourselves, all for the sake of a high. If I could give you a picture of what that felt like, it would go something like this... Go out and find the dirtiest drain you can and clog it up. Then, ask every stranger you come across to spit, vomit, and urinate in that drain. Next, I want you to prepare a meal on that drain, eat it, and immediately roll over in it and go to sleep. That's the kind of low we were at. We got low, so that we could get high.

Now that's a pain pill.

I'd like to draw your attention to the fact that it took two of us to get to this point. Looking back, I don't feel as though I would have done half of those things had I been a solo act in my addiction. Again, I must reiterate that I am solely responsible for my own actions. I do not blame others for the choices I make. What I'm saying here is that because I had someone to look to for encouragement in my actions, someone who could look me in my eye, knowing all of my dirty deeds, and I all of theirs, and still say, "We're fine."

That's what made it worse. It was the soothing comfort and the assurance that we weren't alone, which fueled my all-consuming fire of an addiction.

In our addictions we tend to gravitate towards those who will help us justify and feel good about our actions. I knew full well that my girlfriend selling herself was completely degrading and insulting. Not only to me, but even more so for herself. Day after day, it tore my pride and self-worth into shreds. I can only imagine what it's done to her. I willingly partook in an activity, over and over, that would all but paralyze my dignity, leaving behind overwhelming amounts of disgrace and shame for years to come. All for a temporary mood adjuster, or as the world calls it, a drug.

It gets worse. You see, once I got the drug in my hand and took the first hit. (I smoked the pills on tin foil. They call it chasing the dragon.) Once I took that first hit, I would feel better. At least for a minute or two. I'd be high for a while, but that's not what I'm talking about. I'm talking about feeling better about myself and who I was. And in truth, that's all I was really trying to ease. My own lack of self-worth. That relief only lasted for a moment, and almost immediately after taking that first hit, I'd be upset with myself. Thinking of how weak I was to let a little blue pill control me.

The answer... Take another hit. Then another and another. But no matter how many hits I take, no matter how many lines I snort, no matter how much I drink, it's not enough. It doesn't fix my problem. When the smoke clears, the reality is still the same. I was a lost soul, being carried about in this world like a plastic bag in a tornado.

My life was quite the vicious cycle. It's the same cycle that so many other people have been stuck in. A cycle which wears a mask of joy and happiness but once inside you find that it's filled with torment and anguish. From the outside it looks like everyone's doing it, and if you can just be part of that fun ride, you'll join the club. But once you've entered its doors you find that you're all alone. You get pulled this way and that and can't get a grasp on anything solid or concrete. This cycle has done nothing but give me an abundance of every single thing I was trying to hide and run away from. All of the ugliness in my life was amplified once that cycle got a hold of me. And no matter how hard I looked or how hard I tried, the beauty that I was in search of kept passing me by in a blur.

I've learned, only after being sober, that you have to hate the drug. If you wish to fully conquer the drug you must come to hate it and everything around it. I say that to say this: I've grown to harbor a deep hatred for this cycle. I hate it for not only what it's done to me, but to what it's done and is currently doing to millions of others, including that girl from down the street.

There is only one way that I can articulate or convey that a person can successfully break free of that cycle. But me telling you holds absolutely no bearing unless you are willing to believe. The second you believe what I'm about to tell you is the second the wind stops. The very instant that you start to believe what I'm about to tell you is the very instant change will begin to occur.

Jesus Christ.

Yes, even a person like me. The same guy you just read about for the last three chapters, even he can be accepted by God. Believe that. If you've tried everything else and nothing has worked, please, try Jesus. I am a living testimony.

Remember, we're not so different, you and me. Only the details are what's changed, the truth remains the same. We all share the same struggles.

You're not alone. And just know that the deep pit of misery of addiction can still be climbed out of. There is still hope. In fact, there is only one point in life in which all hope is lost, and that's the grave.

Chapter 5

DUSTY LENSES

In life, there is this ever-present, wonderfully crafted mystery taking place. It happens to each and every one of us. And if you try to make comparisons to someone else's, you can't. This mystery occurs on such an ambiguous and puzzling level that no two instances are alike. And no one person is ever truly able to pin down either its origin or its destination.

What I'm talking about here is something we have all come to know and refer to as an event. Events take place in our lives every single day, every single moment. And though sometimes we may be able to say, clearly, this is happening for such and such reason. But the truth is that many times, we have no idea at all, and more than likely while we think we might have the answer pinned down, we're completely wrong. This is a tough thing for the rational mind of man to grab hold of and accept. We as humans always want to feel as though we know the WHY of something. We always want the security of not being taken by surprise.

But the reality is, in life, many of the events we encounter, their purpose and meaning are far hidden from us. And sometimes an immediate event might not prove its worth or relevance for many years to come.

DECEMBER 2015

"Fifteen years for count two... Fifteen years for count three... Fifteen years for counts four and five. Five years for counts six, seven, and eight..."

These were the judge's words. They came out nonchalantly, in the most calming of tones. It held the same intensity as someone reading off a grocery list to a litter of puppies.

At first I thought that he was just simply reading off the charges and what each one carried. I already knew what I was facing. I wanted to know what my sentence was....

In that moment, something told me to look down at my public pretender's, sorry, I mean public defender's note pad.

It was right there in the center of the yellow page. Written in bold red ink: "15 yrs." And as if that weren't enough, he circled it. He may as well have drawn a smiley face around it.

When you see people in movies falling through a virtual tunnel, that's what I felt like. The world around me had become a deafening blur of muted colors and streaks of light all swirling together. Nothing was left as it should be. Reality had left the building. I was now falling backwards, helplessly floating through some great vacuum of space and time. Nothing mattered.

A few years into my fifteen-year bid, after a streak of rebelliousness and a big middle finger to the authority—we call it "bucking"— I had finally come to accept my fate. I accepted the fact that I was powerless. The fact that my life was no longer my own. My food, my sleep, the clothes I wore, they were all decisions someone else was now making for me. I was no longer responsible for anything other than waking up every day and receiving the free handouts of food rations and hygiene supplies.

Regardless of what you may think, prisons in Florida are not designed to rehabilitate or correct any faulty thinking or behavior. There are little to no self-betterment programs available and even fewer trades. Schooling goes no further than gaining a GED, with the exception of a small handful of locations among the seventy-plus prisons that do offer vocational training, and two locations that offer education at the college level. One of those two will only admit you if you have over fifteen years left on your sentence. And the logic is so that the learned individual can occupy the need of a chaplain on any given compound. So they'll provide education, so long as it benefits the prison. Needless to say I felt as though my life had no purpose.

Nothing I did, no book I read, no number of push-ups, no championship title for, "dorm's best chess player" would help me make any progress in life. I was doing nothing more than being warehoused, filling a space. I couldn't see any reasonable purpose for me being in prison.

This lack of purpose led me right back to what I knew best: drugs. This was insanity; I was going back to doing the very same thing that got me sent to prison in the first place. I may as well have been housed in a psychiatric ward.

In my quest to find the purpose of the current event I was going through, I resorted back to the only thing my mind could quantify as having value and meaning. I thought that being high was the only way of curing my sense of worthlessness, and reversing the curse placed on my life.

Here's where that great mystery came poking its head into the picture. And since I'm a prideful man, I tried to make sense of it all on my own.

This life event that had no apparent meaning or purpose, I tried to assert my own assertion and opinion of what it should produce. What I couldn't see, and what I inevitably learned, was that all of the free time and lack of responsibility was a gift, not a curse.

How many people in the world today go to great lengths and will pay great sums of money and pursue with vigor a freedom from responsibility and time constraints? How many people need nothing more than to just "unplug" from the world? How many people search the world over for a small slice of solitude?

I had all of that. In abundance.

The event of having to serve fifteen years in prison, though I doubt anyone would volunteer for it, had significant worth. A worth that took nearly three years to see.

What situation are you in, or have you gone through that while in the middle of it, it seemed as though its only purpose was to bring you pain and suffering? How many times have you gone through an event that at first appeared to be a bad situation, and later discovered that it was in fact working out for a greater good?

This is where the rubber meets the road for us. I'm talking to the addicts here. This is the part that gravely affects our lives, day in and day out. It's all about THE WAY in which we view, and, subsequently, deal with our various situations and events in life. It's all about cleaning our DUSTY LENSES.

As an addict, we tend to view and filter every situation through a negative lens. Meaning our perception of the world is passed through a negative way of seeing things. This is done for two reasons. And both of those reasons occur on a subconscious level; we do it without even trying.

The first is that we look for an excuse to do drugs. "Because this is a bad situation," or "This situation made me upset" is a good enough reason for us to get high. We've got it fixed in our minds that drugs can solve everything, that drugs will make all of life's problems just go away.

Now the second, more subtle and deceptive reason why we view the world through a negative scope is, are you ready...? It's because of the drugs.

At this point it may seem like I'm just trying to bash drug use. And yes, I am bashing it, with a concrete block right over its head. But that doesn't make what I'm about to tell you any less true.

Drugs do something to our brain that even science has a hard time explaining. I'm not talking about physical effects, or a decrease in brain activity. No, it's something other, and it occurs on a subatomic level, completely undetectable but extremely influential.

Drug use creates this inability to view the world in a positive light. It distorts our powers of detection and perception, taking everything good that happens to us and reversing it. It's as if we see positive and negative through a mirrored image. Every positive thing gets viewed as a negative, and every negative gets viewed as a positive. A sure path to destruction.

Here are some examples...

POSITIVES BEING VIEWED AS NEGATIVES

* If someone offers you a compliment, you more than likely suspect that they are up to something devious.

* If someone tries to do something nice for you, such as give you some money, you'll more than likely be suspicious, or if not, you'll take the money and think of them as being gullible and foolish for doing it. Not able to appreciate the act of kindness for what it truly is.

*If a drug cartel who has killed thousands and left hundreds of thousands homeless, starving, and jailed, because of the drugs they manufacture and sell. If this cartel were to get busted by the FBI we'd rally against the prosecution's case in hopes of them getting freed.

NEGATIVES BEING VIEWED AS POSITIVES

* If your drug dealer agrees to give you credit for some drugs for the full amount of your up-and-coming paycheck, knowing that you won't turn it down, we as addicts see this as a good thing.

* If you find out that people are overdosing on a batch of heroine, we think that's good, and run to go find it.

Drugs have completely shifted our entire moral compass. Up is down, black is white, and right is wrong. This is not the way life was intended to be.

And the reason this happens is so simple, it's scary...because it's all a lie. The drugs take truth, and somewhere in the most inner workings of our brain, it twists it around. Makes us doubt the validity of everything we know. And in the place of truth, it spits out lie after lie, until the only thing you can really be certain of is the drug itself.

Now that we have a firm understanding of why we as addicts view the world the way we do, what next? What do we do with this information? Nothing.

NOTHING!? "I thought this was supposed to help and encourage me?"

It is. Understand that the battle between you and drugs is only a surface metaphor for something much deeper. It is a battle between light and dark. Good and evil. Between God and the devil.

Good will never try to force anything on you. It will not try to make you do anything. Good wants you to enjoy true freedom. It's the equivalent of pure love. So if you choose to do evil, that's your right, that's your freedom of choice. In the same token, as long as you're living a life where you are participating in the enemy's schemes, evil will never try and stop you. Why would it? You're acting as one of its soldiers, carrying out its mission.

But the moment you wake up and realize that you no longer wish to live in darkness, evil will step in and begin to try to assert its dominance over you. It will make you dope sick when you get up in the morning. It will rob you, beat you, and leave you begging for a piece of the miserable life you've been living. It will trick you into thinking that the darkness is where you belong and that change for something better is pure fallacy.

And now here comes the question, "If God loves us, why let the devil win like that?" The answer... He's not, you are.

You have to fully give in to God before he will step in and intervene in your life. You have to fully submit and confess that nothing you've tried to do, or can do, is able to defeat the darkness. You must confess that God is the only way.

That's the stark contrast between the two. It's all the evidence you'll ever need when it comes to doubting God for who He is; it's how you know that God loves you and that the devil hates you. The devil will interrupt your entire life, impose himself even if he's not wanted. God is patient and will give you all of the space you need, never forcing anything on you. But the very second you drop to your knees and acknowledge who He is and how much you need Him and how helpless you truly are against the devil, that's the moment you will finally experience change in your life. Change for the better.

So yes, do nothing. And for once, let God take control. I promise you the God of the universe is much better at problem-solving than we are.

Here's one more thing to reflect on. Think of any relationship you've ever had. Has the other person ever been wrong, about anything? It doesn't matter the details. Just think. What if they never were to admit that they were wrong? If they never were to have swallowed their pride and accepted the fact that you were right, or never would have apologized...?

Think about how that simple act of submission can turn the rockiest and volatile relationship into a good standing one. The Bible tells us that "God resists the proud, but gives grace to the humble."

Rid yourself of pride and replace it with humility. Humble yourself and let go of trying to make sense of the events of your life, we will never be able to see things the way God does. The best thing you can do for yourself is to stop looking at life through the corrupted and distorted lens of the enemy, wipe the dust away, and start seeing it through the clear and concise lens that God has gifted you with.

Chapter 6
FEAR vs. SOUND MIND

"For God has not given us a spirit of fear, but of power and of love and of sound mind." 2 Timothy 1:7

FEAR vs. SOUND MIND

I want to, very briefly, take a look at what the word fear means, where it comes from, and what its purpose is. The dictionary defines it as "an emotion experienced in the presence or threat of danger. To experience concern or worry."

So what are some of the other ways we can describe fear? Alarm, anxiety, fright, terror, panic, phobia, agitation, cowardice. I don't think there is a single person out there who can honestly say that they desire to experience any of those things.

We know now what fear is. What we need to know next is, where does it come from? Think about a child, when they're afraid of a monster in the corner of their room. They run out crying, searching for someone to help them. The parent guides them back to the room and turns on the light. The monster they thought they seen was only a shadow.

Did you catch it? Pay attention. Someone GUIDES them back and TURNS ON THE LIGHT.

Our fear comes from a place of distorted views. (Remember the lenses in which we look through.) Fear lives in shadows, and shadows are completely subject to the will of light. Wherever the light goes, a shadow must follow and conform to what the light does, no matter the amount of light. Whether it be a small beam passing through a hole inside of the shed, or whether the roof be completely pulled back and removed. The light is both dictator and commander of the shadows. Shadow is slave to light.

So what is the purpose of fear? Fear has one goal: CONTROL. Fear wants to control us. It wants to make us a slave to falsehoods, tricks, and deceptions. When we act in the pretenses of fear or under the obscurity of shadows, we cannot possibly be free to make our own decisions.

Here's what I mean... A person who is stricken with terror is usually frozen, both physically and mentally. They're unable to not only think rationally but to form any thought outside of the situation at hand. Hence making that person a slave. Someone who is panicked, they can no longer form a thought or act outside of the situation in which they feel panicked about. A person who is experiencing anxiety has fixed their mind and is fully dwelling on a "shadow" or situation and is not in the least bit able to even muster up a single thought outside of that. Trapped by a shadow, a slave to a slave.

This is the purpose of fear. To stop you from turning on the light and seeing clearly what is truly going on.

Now that we know who and what fear is and its intentions, we're going to discover what a SOUND MIND is.

What does the word SOUND mean in this context? The definition says that it is "Free from defect, decay or damage. In good condition. Marked by or showing common sense and good judgement."

What a contrast. On one hand fear brings about all sorts of defects and the decaying of our minds. And on the other we have a freedom from this.

As always, I want to show you how these things affect us, the addict. Whenever we are sober, we are of a sound mind. In fact the definition for sober is "Devoid of frivolity, excess, exaggeration, or speculative imagination."

So to be sober is the opposite of living in a make-believe world created by our own imaginations (afraid of shadows in the dark). Sober is the absence of frivolousness or wastefulness in our lives.

When you're sober, or of a sound mind, you are now qualified to make judgments. This is the gift that God gives us. It's the ability to decipher what's going on around us and to properly navigate our daily lives without the worry or concern of making mistakes.

Being under the influence of a drug brings about the opposite effect.

There is no stable thinking, we're not firm, and our thoughts are not based in reality, and most definitely not qualified. Tell me what job do you know of will knowingly allow you to operate their machinery and their equipment or deal with their customers while under the INFLUENCE of a drug. None. You become unqualified. Your qualified judgement that God has gifted you with is now unqualified.

Why does this happen? Drugs make you feel good. Why would being under their influence make me an unqualified individual? If they were bad, why would God have created them?

The answer is simple: God didn't create drugs, man created them. I already know what you're thinking, and it's the same argument I've used to try and justify my addiction: "Marijuana grows naturally. So that means God made it, and it's okay for me to use." Yes, this is true, God did create it. But marijuana by itself has no effect. It's the same thing as if you take the natural element sodium (created by God) and mix it with another natural element, chlorine (also created by God). Alone they're not so bad, but when man steps in and tries to perform his own will, it becomes a deadly poisonous gas. The same goes with marijuana: mix it with enough heat, a natural element, and it will cause a smoke, or a gas, however you want to look at it, and this gas has the power to take away your natural, God-given state, a qualified and sound mind. And in exchange, giving you an unqualified, distorted, and discredited mind.

Since we're on the subject of marijuana, I would like to take a side note here and really reflect on what marijuana's whole purpose is.

MARIJUANA

Imagine a neighbor who every time you leave the house, he's out front, smiling and waving. He's always watering the grass and tending to the flowers. He looks like he's got it all figured out and is just enjoying life to the fullest. You've heard all sorts of bad stories about him, and none of them seem true. You decide one day to introduce yourself. You invite him in for some coffee. You guys hit it off. (Pun intended.) He's got you cracking up, laughing at the dumbest jokes, he makes your favorite movie a hundred times more enjoyable, and he shows you how to make fourteen different types of peanut butter and jelly sandwiches.

You think to yourself, *this guy is great, he's like my best friend.* You introduce him to your other friends. They hit it off. He's a big hit at parties and trips to the beach, you two have the same taste in music, and he shows you a deeper meaning to life's greatest questions. Like, why do you drive on a parkway and park on a driveway? (Yeah, that just happened.)

Then, one day, you two are sitting there in the living room watching cartoons and you realize, *dang, man, I was supposed to be at work yesterday.* Oh no, and today! He tells you it's all right, he assures you that your boss won't mind. Everything will be okay. You trust him. And why wouldn't you? He's a great guy.

A week passes and you get a phone call telling you that you've missed too many days, come in and pick up your paycheck. You're fired. You freak out and panic; this last month alone you've spent way too much money on video games and delivery food. How are you going to pay the rent?

He starts to tell you about his brother and sister who live next door with him. And how they can help you make some quick cash. Their names are pills and cocaine.

We all know how this story ends. We've seen it a hundred times. And it will never change. We will always meet the friendly and relatable marijuana first, and once the weed has broken down our defenses and left us vulnerable, in comes the rest of it.

Let's go back to the analogy of the kid who's afraid of the dark. There was a very important piece to that puzzle we haven't visited yet. And that's the part where they RUN for help, and someone GUIDES them back.

You've heard me say already that you cannot overcome this battle on your own. The roots to your "drug tree" run far too deep. If you want to see clearly, if you want the light turned on, if you want to be sober, you must RUN for help.

That means to go out in haste. Do not delay. Be expedient. The longer you lie there, focusing in on the shadows, the more you begin to believe the lie being presented to you. Get up right now and run to the helper.

In your hastiness and urgency, the one in which you've run to will recognize how critical this is for you. They will recognize the desperation. You'll take on an air of transparency and vulnerability. All of the boundaries and walls you've worked your whole life to build will come tumbling down, allowing the spirit of truth to flow and deal with the issue at hand. And most importantly, through your honesty in what it is you're dealing with, you open yourself up to a willingness to be guided.

Pay attention to the word *guide*. It requires something from you. I can't guide you if you're not willing to move with me. And if you're not careful, it's at this point that you might see another shadow and take off running away from the guide. There's one more lie waiting for you at this exact point in your quest for sobriety. It's there in that moment, when you're so close, waiting like the cunning and crafty serpent it is, to whisper these words, "You don't have the strength to move. You don't have the courage to go. If you follow them, you'll be a fool. You'll be weak."

Lies. All of it. The truth is that if you've made it to the point of running to someone for help, then you've already showed the strength to move. You've already displayed the courage to go. And you've already overpowered the weakness and made a fool of the shadow's paralyzing grip of fear.

When discussing fear, there's another aspect of it that people usually don't like to talk about. In fact, it's the portion of fear that people shy away from the most and do everything in their power to ignore it altogether. Psychologists will classify this aspect as a lack of self-confidence or insecurity. But as one speaking from experience, and not book work, I'd call it the fear of being yourself.

2002 Terry Parker High School, Jacksonville, FL

"You're actually going to school today?" this kid asked me. I don't remember his name. If I were to see him today, I wouldn't even recognize him. But for some reason, he took up a whole lot of space in my head. Maybe because I wanted to be like him. He was, after all, one of "the cool kids." Not a football jock, not a popular kid. But a cool kid. He smoked pot and cigarettes, drank liquor, had a girlfriend that put out, and he didn't give a damn about anything. And I wanted to be just like him.

"Psh, yeah right," I told him, changing my mind from what I had initially planned on doing, which was go to school. "I'm just looking for the right person to skip with. I don't need no lame dragging me down."

"You can ride with me. I got the whip and the blunts. All you need is the weed."

That was the blueprint for how my second year in the ninth grade went. Wasted.

My life was spent chasing after other people and trying to fit their mold of what they saw as an "acceptable guy." I was always under the impression that I was either missing out on something or that what I was doing had no value.

I didn't even like my own name. The only place I found any value was in other people's lives and partaking in and furthering their agendas, not mine.

Only now am I able to properly identify this as a fear. I was afraid that if I spent time on me, then I would discover who I was.

Let me say that again. I was afraid that if I spent time on me, I would discover who I was.

What's wrong with that, you ask? The fear lay not in the fact that I would discover who I was, but once I knew, I wouldn't like what I found. I was afraid that the true me would be an ugly, foul, and decrepit person. I was afraid that the qualities I would find, would be all the ones I hated.

This type of fear is one of the most dangerous ones there is to an addict. In a world (the drug world) where people are always looking to find their next mark and someone to leech off of, this places you at a high risk.

If I can take your energy and time and use it for my own needs, I have just doubled up on my efficiency. Two people carrying out the same task. Not only that, but you, as the one being used, made little to no progress in your own life. In fact, your life is being put on hold so long as you are living for someone else's purposes.

Think about this. You skip school just to appease someone else. You fail that grade. You pick your spouse based upon what others think, you'll end up miserable and in a relationship you loath. You slack off at your job or stop going all together because of someone else's opinion or desire; you become unemployed and broke. You do drugs because the cool kid does them; you become an addict.

Remember, I'm not just talking, I've lived this.

As I grew and became more deeply addicted to drugs, this fear of being myself got worse and worse, all the while growing more and more subtle. I began to care about useless stuff. Things that were pure distractions from what really mattered in life. Things like what kind of shoes I wore, or how new they were. I could be at the register paying for a 150-dollar pair of tennis shoes, and once I walked away, the ones on the wall seemed to be a better choice.

I was the kind of addict that wanted to do the most drugs out of everyone I knew. And I wanted everyone to know that I was top drug addict on the yard. I had it pinned down in my mind that this was a badge of honor, something too revered.

I gave you an example of what this fear looks like for good reason, but first, let's look at it from one more angle. At this point any halfway educated person would be saying, "This sounds exactly like insecurities." That's because it is insecurity.

But let's look at the word insecure. The root word there is secure. To be secure means safe or at ease. So its opposite, insecure, would mean lacking security. Unsafe.

If you are lacking security or if you're feeling unsafe, it's because of a FEAR. For instance, if you left the front door open, you would only feel unsafe or unsecured if a FEAR of an intruder was present. But if you lived in the middle of a fortress or on the top of a highly guarded mountain, there would be no fear of someone intruding. And your door being open would no longer leave you with any insecurities.

So where fear ceases to exist, so does our insecurity. And in its place, we find security. Once we attack the fear and rid ourselves of it, all of our insecurities will go with it, leaving us with a clean slate. A life full of freedoms to do as we please and not as the next person pleases.

And lastly, if you decide to leave your door open, and you do it without fear, you do it because of the sense of freedom and joy you get from the things you like. An outside breeze, sunshine, whatever your reason. But now you do it, knowing who you are.

It's the same way with living to help others and dedicating our lives to the promotion of other people's happiness. When we do it from a state of fear, because we don't know who we are, it makes us a slave. But when we know who we are and we willingly live for others in a state where there is no fear present, we do it with that same sense of freedom and joy.

The enemy will always TRY and turn what God intends for good and use it for evil. And God will always SUCCEED at taking what the enemy meant for evil and use it for good.

You didn't think I was going to tell you about this wonderful way of living and not show you how to achieve it, did you?

It's not a step-by-step process. There aren't any scientifically proven methods. There's no clinical research to be expounded upon. The only thing you need is a small seed of belief.

Without further ado, allow me to introduce you to the person who helped me, and millions of others, to discover who we are in this life. The person who helped us to break through the fear. The person who turned the light on in the midst of our darkest hour. He's the beginning and the end. The Alpha and the Omega. He's the way, the truth, and the light. He's the King of kings and the Lord of lords. He's both the Shepherd and the Lamb. He's the lion of Judah. Almighty Yahweh. The great I AM. He's the creator of the entire universe, and He's my best friend. His name is Jesus.

Chapter 7

THINK NEGATIVELY

"I knew it, this guy has no idea what he's talking about. He just got done telling us to wipe away our dusty lenses. Now he starts this chapter with THINK NEGATIVELY."

That's exactly what I would be thinking if I was still an addict. And since I have an addict's mind... But here's what I mean by this: THINK NEGATIVELY in regard to the drugs.

For instance, if you're standing next to a cluster of trees and there's all sorts of foliage and shrubs grown up around you preventing you from being able to see past the few feet of your immediate vicinity, can you accurately say that you are in a forest? How big of a forest? Or is it just a patch of woods? You can assume that you're standing in a forest, but in actuality, you're too close to gain an accurate view of the situation.

Now, once you're removed and are able to stand afar off and look back at where you once were, then you can positively say with conviction and surety that it was in fact a forest. And not just any forest, but now you can see the specifics. It's a national forest located in the Ozark Mountains, with a log cabin off in the clearing.

Another way to look at it is to take a penny and hold it as close to your eye as you can. The penny, when it's up close and it's the only thing you can see, is huge. It's the size of a house. But once you pull it back, now you can gain the proper perspective, putting it in its place as a penny and nothing more. This is what we are trying to do here. To take a step back from our current situation and gain a more accurate idea of what we're dealing with. I want to start with this quote I once heard: "The Christ that lives in you is bigger than the crisis that lives around you."

AUGUST 2020 Okeechobee Prison, FL

We all know that 2020 was the year of pandemonium. With hate-inspired riots, a media that filled our heads with lies, and a contagious virus which swept across the world in a swift and devastating fashion, this particular year was filled with a spirit of fear and confusion. And we all fell victim, one way or another.

During all of this, I was at a place in my life where I was actually practicing good habits. I was several months sober, working out and exercising every day, reading my Bible and other books. I even finished writing the last few chapters of a novel. I had finally found a positive lifestyle within the prison system.

Meanwhile, all around me that spirit of fear and confusion was hard at work. Everywhere I looked were guys using and selling drugs. Daily, hour by hour. In fact, this particular prison I was at was one of the most corrupt and contraband-filled prisons I had ever seen. And the dorm I lived in was the hub of it all. There was even major wine production going on which pumped out about forty gallons a week. Shot caller upon shot caller, gang leaders and crime bosses. And whatever your drug-using heart desired, they had it.

So here I am, doing everything in my power to stay sober, and all I see is the opposite. I felt as though I was the only one trying to live right. I felt like an outcast. As I looked on at all of the guys doing drugs, drinking, making money, having a blast, I couldn't help but long for that same old feeling.

I gave in. It started with me deciding to sell the stuff. I worked it out in my mind that this was an adequate way of staying relevant. It was my way of having the cake and eating it too. I didn't want to be controlled by drugs anymore, but controlling people with drugs was all right... But an addict will always be an addict.

After the third batch, I started using again. Moderately at first, but as we know, an addict does nothing in moderation. Soon enough it came to a point where I would only sell just enough to pay my dealer so I could re-up. I thought that I was a somebody, but all I was doing was spinning my wheels, trying to stay afloat. And before long, I was no longer selling any of it. I was a full-blown customer, and a full-blown addict. Back like I never left.

There was one single point, one defining moment, in all of that where I went wrong. Some might say that trying to sell the stuff was where I went wrong. Yes, that was the action that I took which led me right back into the grips of addiction. But the moment of error came even before that. My first mistake was not the drug, it was the way I THOUGHT about the drug.

THINK NEGATIVELY

You've heard over and over to think positively. You've been told that if you think positive, then you'll get positive results. And this is true. But not when it comes to an addict trying to overcome their addiction.

When you see people doing drugs, the first thing that goes through your head is all of the enjoyable times you had. Your mind takes you back to all of the favorable memories. The parties, the romances, the dancing, and laughing.

Your vision is completely obscured; you're standing in the cluster of trees, and the penny is too close to your eye. I can guarantee you, if nothing else, this one thing: it's not fun. For every one enjoyable memory, you have ten that haunt you.

When I look back on this chapter of my life, I realize that the best thing I could have done was to think negatively. Instead of noticing the smile and happiness while they were scoring the dope, I should have been paying attention to the look they had before they got the money. I should have paid attention to the misery they were in when they were broke and had no idea where they would get their next hit from.

Instead of watching them for the first few moments after they took that hit, and seeing that all-familiar look of intoxicating bliss and delight on their face, I should have waited. Just a little patience and what I would have found was the complete opposite. The high would have worn off, and an exchange would have taken place. Delight in exchange for discomfort, elation, and euphoria for irritation and sorrow, and bliss in exchange for misery.

Who knows where we as addicts would be if we could just get this one thing right. Maybe we wouldn't get lured into dark alleys. Or the commercial for our favorite liquor wouldn't make us clutch our car keys. We might be able to last a whole day with our paychecks. And perhaps, every time we give a shot at sobriety, we wouldn't get knocked flat on our faces.

So stop repressing the hurt and the pain drugs have caused you. Remember it. Keep it in the front of your mind. Remember the nights you spent hungry. Remember the looks on your kids' faces when they found out. Remember the gut punch you felt every time your kids wanted, better yet needed new shoes, and instead you chose to give the money to a drug dealer. Remember all the times you did something for money that you're either too ashamed to tell about, or if you did, you'd end up in prison. Remember every lie you've told to people you love. Remember all of the hurt you've caused. The broken homes. The shattered lives. The attempts at suicide. Even worse, the success of suicide.

There is no happy ending. Not as long as we continue to ignore the bad times. There will never be a cleansing if we don't grow to hate the drug. That is the only way you'll ever be able to quit. If we don't start THINKING NEG-ATIVELY, we'll be doomed and destined for destruction.

The drug is not our friend. It does not wish us any wellbeing in our lives. The drug comes cloaked and shrouded in deceit and deception. It's time we yank the cloak away and see it for what it is.

A destroyer.

Chapter 8
TRUTH and LIES

Before you get into this chapter, I would be remised if I didn't present you with a disclaimer first. If you are not ready to have your beliefs rocked to the core, do not read past this point. But if a TRUE change in your life is what you are after, please, by all means...

From the very moment you came into this world until now, and even until the day you die, you will be at war. A continuous battle will be waged. Day in and day out you will be engaged in a struggle, an all-out brawl, punches, kicks, eye gouging, chokeholds, arm bars, you name it. And you won't even realize it.

Truth and Lies. Pay close attention here; notice that the word "Truth" is singular, and "Lies" is plural. The Truth consists of one single element. A lie has many. In fact, its very origin is one of division. It seeks to divide instead of unite. It cares nothing about justice or what's right. You may have never thought of it in this way, but a Lie has its own agenda. There is always an ulterior motive....

AUGUST 2015

I was sitting in the county jail facing a slew of charges and trying to come to grips with the reality that I was going to end up doing some serious time. I had a cellmate who was in for a simple misdemeanor. All he was waiting on was a court date and would probably receive time served and be released. And as bunkies usually do in jail and in prison, we talked. Night after night, every day the only thing on his mind was what he planned to do once they let him out. I ignored its validity for the first week; this was jail, and people lie. But then, something happened one night... "I have to hurry up and get back out," he said.

"Stop crying. You got nothing but some misdemeanors. You're getting out real soon," I said.

"I can't let this bitch put me in prison," he said. This wasn't said to me, he mumbled it to himself from the bottom bunk. And this is when I knew he wasn't joking or just talking gangster, trying to sound cool.

"You're serious."

He jumped up. "I'm dead serious. I have to find a way to kill both her and her daughter. If not, I'm going to prison for a long time."

"What did you do that they wanted to send you to prison?"

"That doesn't matter. I just can't let them snitch me out."

"How old is the daughter?" I asked. He kept his eyes on me for a brief moment. They were bright blue, but still found a way to hold the darkness.

"Nine," he said. I couldn't believe it. I didn't respond verbally, I couldn't. I was speechless, but I know that my face conveyed perfectly just how sick I felt. I lay down and couldn't fall asleep for a long time after that; I just stared up at the ceiling.

Nine years old. I thought about my cousin and his daughter. I thought back to when I was sixteen and my own sister was nine. How precious they were. I imagined if my sister had kids. If I had kids. I didn't know what the reason for wanting to kill the girl and her mother was, but it's like he said, it didn't even matter.

I wanted to do something. I had to do something. There come moments in our lives when we get this heavy impression upon us, urging, begging us to take some action. This was one of those times. And as I walked through my options, none of them had any form of resolution at the end of its path.

Beat him up. He'll still get out and kill those people. Kill him. He won't kill those people but I will have guaranteed myself a life sentence. There was only one option left. And this is where my lifelong battle between TRUTH and LIES came into play.

Growing up I was always taught to never snitch. Don't tell. Take it to your grave. This was a concept I had adopted, enforced, and strongly stood behind. I had a shirt with a stop sign and the word snitching in the middle of it. The song "Snitch" by a top rapper was among my favorites. Society as a whole looks down on this very act. And here I was, actually contemplating it.

I wrestled for a few days over this. It affected my whole life. I wasn't sleeping, I barely ate. And all the while having to look this guy in the face and hide my disgust and contempt for him. I was in a serious battle. Right was right and wrong was wrong. But what I was always taught to be wrong, at this moment, was the right thing to do.

I don't know exactly what it was that helped push me to make the final decision, but I went to the prosecutor and told them of this guy's plan. That if they let him out, he would kill a girl and her mother. They tried to get me to testify and wear a wire on him in exchange for a time reduction. I told them I wanted nothing else to do with it, that they had all the info they needed and to do what they deem necessary.

I was liberated. No longer did I feel guilty about not taking any action. No longer did the fate of two innocent people weigh on my conscience. I was finally able to get a good night's rest once again.

For the record, there is a difference between doing what's right and telling on someone in order to avoid your own punishment. If you were caught for something, be a man and accept your just due. Also, if you try and use the justice system to your benefit, such as *if I tell on this drug dealer, I can get all of his territory or clients*, that's just as wrong. But righting a wrong, putting an end to someone's evil for the sole purpose of it being the right thing to do, that is the difference.

In addition, I received no favor from the courts, no money was put in my account, nothing. In fact, I received the maximum sentence that my charges carried.

This is an area in which the enemy has triumphed for far too long. Society as a whole has this picture in their mind that any form of informing is wrong. That's a LIE concocted by Satan himself. He wants nothing more than to trick people into allowing evil to go unpunished. I'll say that again, Satan wants you to assist him in making sure evil goes unpunished.

Nowhere in the Bible will you find that God prohibits people from informing authorities of an evil that is or has taken place. What He does say is that if you bring a charge against someone, it had better be true. You will never see where God has told the human race *if you see someone get murdered, keep your mouth shut.* If someone breaks into your house and steals everything you have, don't call the cops. Never. God is just and true. In fact, here are only a small portion of the scriptures where we are not only commanded to do this, but also how it affects our relationship with God when we do what's right...

Proverbs 17:15: "He who justifies the wicked and he who condemns the just, both of them alike are an abomination to the Lord."

Proverbs 11:1: "Dishonest scales are an abomination to the Lord, but a just weight is His delight."

Proverbs 18:5: "It is not good to show partiality to the wicked, Or to overthrow the righteous in judgement."

John 7:7: "...The world hates me because I testify of its works that they are evil."

What has happened is that man has adopted this concept that we are the deciding factor in what's right and what's wrong. We have created our own set of laws outside of Gods. We are right and God is wrong. We know better than God. Basically.

To add injury to insult, not only have we completely disregarded God's sovereign authority, we have, in the process of coming up with our own laws, set in place a punishment should you actually follow God's law. We then took it a step further and insisted that in the event that you do follow God's law and put a stop to our evil, then it's perfectly just and okay to violate God's law and kill you. Or at best, simply injure you. Snitches get stitches. We even came up with a clever catch phrase.

Are you starting to see how a lie we've been led to believe can tow a whole trailer full of ulterior motives behind it? Something as simple as Don't Snitch. A lie so evil that if you believe and pattern your life after it, it will have you beating down the front door to hell and pushing everyone out the way so that you can get there first.

Here's the good news: humans are born with supernatural abilities. We can sense things that are outside of the scope of the five senses. It can't be seen, heard, smelled, touched, or tasted. But we know it's there. The things which we're talking about are principalities, ideas, concepts, but even more specifically, TRUTH AND LIES.

As an addict we lack clarity. We lose the ability to discern and comprehend basic principles. We can no longer sense the effects of these invisible things;

the line between truth and lies has become so blurred that we often mingle and mix the two. They become interchangeable as we see fit. It becomes a thing we try to use and manipulate, regardless of never actually being in control of these forces to begin with.

When we think that we can shape the lie or bend the truth, we only fool ourselves. A lie will trick you into believing that because you can alter it as you see fit, you are the one using and controlling it. You hold all of the cards. That the only reason you lied was to suit yourself. That's a lie all on its own, you just don't know it. The lie has so craftily hidden its ulterior motive, its true nature, that you don't even realize that the lie is the one using you. That as you go about telling lies you are only furthering the enemy's agenda.

When we lie, it sets in motion a long line of future lies. Forcing us to return to it over and over again. We become its slave. It leaves us uncomfortable, always on edge. We're not sure whether or not we'll be found out and put to shame. If and when we're confronted with the lie we've told, we go on the defensive. It has the ability to tear apart relationships and families. It has the ability to falsely send a person to the death penalty. Nothing but destruction is left in the wake of a lie. Is that not the work of an enemy?

If you had a bowl of glass in front of you, and you were led to believe that it was in fact cereal, what would happen? You would bite into it and instantly realize that what was told to you was a lie. You would feel betrayed, angered, thoughts of revenge would flare up. And if I wanted you to continue on eating the bowl of glass, I would have to come up with an even bigger lie to keep you going. "That's not pain you feel. It's just flavor bursting inside of your mouth."

The truth would have stopped all of that. You would have never gotten cut, your gums wouldn't be bleeding, and you would still be able to depend on me.

I can't even begin to tell you just how many times I've accepted a lie and carried out my life according to that lie. Drugs being one of the biggest ones. "They will make me happy. Drugs will take all my cares away. Being high is the only way I can cope with this world and the people in it." Then when I come to the realization that those were just lies, I'm so full of shame that I tell myself another lie... "Getting high will take my shame away."

Every time I get high, I have to tell myself another lie, and another one, and another one, until my whole existence has become nothing but a lie.

Imagine if you lived your whole life under the pretense of a lie. Everything you did, every action you took, every relationship you had would all be a charade. A house built on sand. And the second the sands began to shift, your entire life would shift with it.

However, the Truth never changes. The Truth won't make you feel uncomfortable or full of shame. In fact, it produces the opposite, self-worth and confidence to begin with. Once you tell the truth, there won't be any chains holding you to it, forcing you to have to go back and try to cover it up. It gives you the freedom to move on with your life. The Truth is not a trick, there's no swindle, it's not a hoax, there's nothing artificial about it. If you pick it up it won't spill through your fingers. The Truth is dependable; it's accurate and reliable.

So how do we break free of this vortex of lies? How do we discern what's true and what's not? By acknowledging the very first Truth. God.

Let's look at a few of the ways the Bible describes the God of truth...

Deuteronomy 32:4: "He is the rock, His work is perfect for all his ways are justice, a God of truth and without injustice."

By Him being a God of truth, this makes for all His work to be perfect and all of his ways to be just. Let's look at some of His perfect works, starting with the earth and man: The plants require the carbon dioxide we exhale, and we require the oxygen that the plants exhale. Perfection. The four elements of this planet—earth, wind, water, and fire. Think of the four things you require to live. Air, water, food (earth), and fire. Yes, fire, because without the perfect temperature we'd all either freeze to death or burn. Perfection.

If there were ever a lie to be found anywhere in God, you could kiss goodbye the perfection of the universe. The distance between the earth and the sun would be something other than what it is, and we'd all be dead. And if in the event that the planets did happen to fall in just the right spot, with just the right tilt and spin, just the right amount of weight and gravity, if that did happen by chance, and humans just so happened to be formed with such precision as we have been, would we be so lucky for the rest of our needs to be met? What about principles like love and justice? What about math? One plus one will always be two.

But what if truth wasn't the basis of life? Could you still rely on math to be unchangeable? Would those things ever have been able to become established without truth? Absolutely not. But because God is truth, all of those things exist.

Psalm 25:5: "Lead me in Your truth and teach me..."

Without the truth, how can you ever expect to learn? If you wish to learn how to tie a knot, and you were taught with a lie, you would have learned a false way of tying a knot, and your knot would always come undone. If you tried to learn how to wire an electrical socket and a lie was involved anywhere in the process, chances are you'd get electrocuted.

Psalms 33:4–5: "For the word of the Lord is right, and all His work is done in truth. He loves righteousness and justice."

Proverbs 12:19: "The truthful lip shall be established forever, but a lying tongue is but for a moment."

John 8:31–32: "If you abide in my word, you are my disciple indeed. And you shall know the truth, and the truth shall make you free."

What does Jesus mean by that? Is Jesus suggesting that He's the truth? Absolutely. But it's not a suggestion, it's a statement. And once you know Him, He will make you free.

The two biggest lies ever to have been uttered by any tongue, past, present, and future, is first, God is not real. And the second is that "He doesn't operate in the life of someone like me, a sinner."

I know, because I've been led to believe both of those throughout my life. But let's not focus on the lie, let's examine truth for a moment. The truth is that no matter who you are or what you've done, God is not only real, but He's in control, and is intimately involved in our lives. And even more importantly, He loves us. And how do we know this to be true? By God's word, the word of the God of truth.

Romans 5:8: "God demonstrates His own love toward us, in that while we were still sinners, Christ died for us."

This one Truth, if you meditate on it, will unravel all of the lies ever told in all of history. Why? Because God is just and True. And because God is love.

Chapter 9
JOSH'S STORY

Sitting in a confinement cell within a Florida prison, withdrawing for the seemingly millionth time from Suboxone—chain gang heroin—a kite came through my flap by way of one of the runarounds serving breakfast trays. It was a message from one of the only people that still stood by me, my wife.

The anticipation killed me. I nearly tore the paper trying to get it opened. I was in desperate need for someone to validate my victim mentality, and who better than my wife. But when I read the words, they were nothing like I had expected. "I can't tell you what your problem is," she said, "only that your unwillingness to address whatever it is will be the death of you."

Immediately I became defensive. Unwilling? Doesn't she know I'm dying here? A twelve-year sentence in prison. Years of that sentence spent in a cell on an isolation unit. I lost my children to this addiction, my freedom, everything. And her only words to me were that I was unwilling to do the work to change.

Like I said, not what I had expected. But I took my wife at her word. After all, she knows better than anyone on this planet. So with nowhere left to turn and my entire existence reduced to yet another six-by-eight-foot confinement cell, I got on my knees and cried out to God, "Please make me willing, show me what's wrong, Father. Save me."

Within moments a thought came to me: The Bible was written and put in a specific order for a reason, I'm sure. Maybe if I read it through, in order, then by the time I get through to Revelation, I might receive just that, a Revelation. After all, that is what I needed. A life-saving, life-changing revelation. So, I began my journey through the story of a chosen people, a people chosen by God Almighty.

I sat in that confinement cell for thirty-eight days. Through the spirit of perseverance, determination, and willingness, I was led through His Word, and at last received that Revelation I so badly needed. The root of my problem, the key ingredient the enemy had been using my entire life to poison me, the active ingredient in his deadly potion, and the foundational element of ruin that was so craftily used and orchestrated in my life was none other than Abandonment.

ABANDONED

Born to a woman with a crack addiction, whose main objective in life was to stay high no matter the cost, I felt as though my only existence was to take care of her, and my two younger siblings, and, of course, myself. I was the responsible one, I was the man of the house. And I was eight years old.

Where there should have been nurturing, love, protection, safety, and compassion, there was violence, hatred, self-seeking and selfishness. Where there should have been family game nights and memorable dinners around a table, instead there was fighting, prostitution, abuse of all kinds—sexual, physical, mental, and emotional. It was a life that no child should ever have to experience. Instead of being taught to love and express affection, I was taught to survive in a world full of grown men that sold or used drugs and would do whatever necessary to achieve their objective.

This was the pattern of my life up until the age of ten; it was at this point that things took a change for the better, but it was already too late for me. The damage had been done.

But let's see the exact event that took place which left permanent scar tissue over my emotions.

JACKSONVILLE, FL 1995

"Hey, Joshua. Come in here, my son. I need to ask you something."

I walked into her room, away from my little brother and sister. "Yeah, Mom?"

"What happened last night?"

Immediately tears filled my eyes. She just looked at me with an empty stare. She didn't have the same light my brother and sis had. Something was missing.

The night she was inquiring about was the one that sticks out most in my mind when I think of my mom. She was out driving around town with her three kids in tow. And as usual, she was wasted.

It was the most terrifying experience. She sped through red lights, had half a dozen near wrecks with oncoming traffic, and even more curb jumps. And the whole time she wore this glazed over expression of joy. I say glazed over because it was nothing like the joy my baby sister had when we played airplane with the spoon. No, my mom's joy, even at the age of ten, I could tell was pure counterfeit.

It was about two a.m. when she finally came to stop at a gas station. I told her I'd steal a beer for her. But as soon she stopped, I jumped out and ran inside. She cussed me and called me all sorts of names. A worthless coward being among them.

I begged the cashier to help me. I told her about the immediate danger me and my two siblings were in. The cops were called. And as always, my mom somehow got out of going to jail. My aunt showed up and took us all back home.

Abandoned: something which was or is useful that has been left unattended, discarded, or forgotten. I thought it would be a good idea to provide you with this definition.

As kids we we're all taught that we're important. That we're special. Somewhere along the lines we've heard it said that we were loved, but when you have been left unattended, when you have been discarded, it's nearly impossible to assimilate this ideology.

Let me give you an example... Let's say you were born blind. You have never seen anything, no colors, no light, not a single shape or shadow. Nothing but pure blackness. You can understand the concept of sight, but the reality of it remains worlds apart. In fact, when a person explains what a thing looks like, they may as well be speaking Greek. So when a child who has experienced nothing but abandonment is told that they are important, it's like telling a blind man what a moving car looks like. He can hear it, he can feel its vibration, he might even be able to smell the oil and burning tires, but he has no idea what it looks like.

It's nothing more than a concept for the blind. I'll take it a step further, and say motion, the very act of motion is nothing more than a feeling on their skin or whooshing in their ears. So what happens? The blind man continues on in life as if the moving car is an appealing idea, a concept that makes sense, but the total reality of it is completely lost to him.

It's interesting, the number of actions we as people regurgitate. I experienced nothing but abandonment, so in return, all throughout my life, I would abandon one thing after another. Starting with my innocence and my childhood. It was because of the imposed responsibilities that I would do this. I had to be the man of the house; that means there was no room for fun and games.

Let's say you had a dog named Fluffy, and you've had him for a few years. Fluffy has gotten used to comfy couches and eating at a regular time every day. Along with belly scratches and games of fetch.

Now drop Fluffy off fifty miles away and leave him there. At first he would feel sad and confused. Fluffy would wander around trying to figure out what this strange new world was. But only so much time would pass before Fluffy, who was abandoned, would have to abandon a few things itself.

No longer can Fluffy wait on feeding time. He now has to go and find his own food. No longer can Fluffy rely on his favorite spot on the couch for comfort. Now he has to try and find a secluded corner that he can feel safe in. Belly scratches and games of fetch? More like gut kicks and car dodging.

Do you see how one simple act of abandonment will force you to abandon everything of your own? This is extremely dangerous for the addict.

The moment you start doing drugs, you, too, are abandoning something. Whether it be happiness, success, your family. Every time we do drugs, we are abandoning something along the way. Take a moment to think of all those things that you have abandoned. How many of them now hold resentment against you. How many of them are now an enemy to you?

Let's just go with sobriety, since its level playing ground for every addict. We have all abandoned sobriety in exchange for a high. Is sobriety now your enemy? Yes, the answer is yes.

Don't believe me, wake up and try to go through the day without getting high. Sobriety will attack you. Sobriety will do everything it can to run and hide from you. Sobriety will give you headaches, it will raise your stress level, give you anxiety, fill you with anger, make you depressed, and the list goes on.

Money. You do drugs, you have abandoned money. It is now your enemy. Try and pay your light bill, buy groceries, fill your gas tank. Money is trying to elude you because you have abandoned it and deemed it worthless.

Your family... Do we even have to go into this one?

As soon as you abandon something or someone, you have made them your enemy. How many enemies can you stand to have? And for what, a drug...? That would be the equivalent of me abandoning my cute and polite golden retriever for a wild and ferocious lion.

All is not lost though. There is hope.

Joshua 1:5: "...I will not leave you nor forsake you."

This is God's promise. But that's not the only promise He makes to us. Let's see what else God has to say about those of us who have been abandoned.

Isaiah 49:15: "Can a woman forget her nursing child and not have compassion on the son of her womb? Surely they may forget, yet I will not forget you."

Wow! I mean, just wow...

When I came across this verse, it broke me down. Uncontrollable tears started falling. You've heard it said that we sometimes cry tears of joy, well, I'm here to tell you that that would only be possible if you first had pain. The tears are inspired by the joy, but the pain is still trapped in those salty drops. The joy is the mechanism used to cleanse the pain away. And it came straight from God's mouth.

Remember, you can only be abandoned if at some point you belonged to someone. Think about that. You belong. And although the mother forgot you, God never will.

Chapter 10
WITCHCRAFT

This is the chapter where we start to "stick it to the man." This one is the big "middle finger" to the powers that be. This is the chapter that US prisons, courtrooms, police forces, and big pharma don't want you to read. This is the part where we really begin to ruffle some feathers and rattle some cages. And to be honest, if I had a big enough platform, I'd probably end up dead because of what I'm about to say...

I also must present you with this warning: After reading this chapter, one of two things will happen. Either you will continue to use drugs and feel even worse than you did before, or you'll make the decision to stop for good. So, continue at your own risk...

Somewhere right now is a person who is willing to commit suicide rather than take one more pill or live one more day on this earth struggling with their addiction. Somewhere right now in this very moment, someone's dying of an overdose. Today someone will get sentenced to fifteen years because of their addiction. Somewhere, right now, a mother, a daughter, a spouse, has just walked into the room to find the person they love, dead, with an empty pill bottle next to them or a syringe in their arm. And somewhere, right now, is a group of people making a fortune off all of that misery.

While those CEOs are enjoying a night out with their family eating dinner at a five-star restaurant and tucking their kids in at night telling them they love them with a kiss on the cheek, their customers have to meet on weekends at visitation, eating food from a vending machine, and can only tell each other they love them over the phone before the time runs out. While they get chauffeured around in luxury sedans trailed by security, their customers get driven around in a hearse trailed by a precession of loved ones.

"It's not the drug company's fault that people are overdosing or going to prison. Their decisions are what led them to either the grave or the prison cell." True. But what if the drug companies produced the drug with the fore-knowledge of what their drug would do to a person? Would that change your perception any? Do you think that for one minute they have released these pain meds into society and had no idea of how addictive they were? Do you think that they weren't aware of the side effects of their drugs? Isn't that what millions of dollars in trials and experiments are for? Do you know that an anxiety pill (a barbiturate) has a possible side effect of kleptomania? It's true. Do they advertise it with this side effect on the label? Of course not. That would be bad for business. But ask anyone who's ever taken that drug, they'll tell you how they woke up with property and money that wasn't theirs. And the worst part is, you wake up with absolutely no recollection of how it happened. Good luck defending yourself in court.

If that weren't enough, there is a drug out there which is supposed to HELP heroin addicts shake their addiction and come off the dope. It works by blocking the opiates from having an effect on the person. So, does it work? I can't say for sure. But that's only because the HELPFUL drug becomes a whole new addiction all on its own. The high is nearly identical, but with an even more increasing level of tolerance build-up than heroin. Meaning, the amount it took to get you high today would be doubled, if not tripled, in a week or two's time. It has almost just as many of the same effects and withdrawal symptoms as heroin does. It's just as hard of a drug habit to kick as the old one. They're more or less imitating the illegal street drug and providing you with a legal alternative. This company could have chosen any number of diseases or ailments to provide medicine for—cancer, leukemia, AIDS, anything. Instead, they've decided to target a very specific demographic, the heroin addict. If they made a commercial it would go something like this... "If you like heroin, then you'll love our new product..."

From a marketing standpoint, a person who is addicted to heroin is the ideal customer. They not only have an expensive habit and come up with creative ways to support it, but they're a loyal and continuous sort of customer. Returning day after day, for years. This drug company has successfully taken hold of the heroin clientele and shifted them over to their own product. What they have done is no different than what nearly every other company does: create a competing product in a competitive market.

And because of the efforts of these companies, for every one person addicted to heroin, there are ten addicted to prescription drugs. The word "pharmacy" comes from the Greek word *pharmakeia*, which means, magic, sorcery, and WITCHCRAFT.

When you imagine or envision a witch, what are they doing? Stirring a cauldron, mixing in different ingredients in hopes of creating the perfect potion. And the purpose of a potion? To, in some way, control the person in which takes or ingests the said potion. Sounds a lot like a scientist in a lab coat trying to find just the right ratio of ingredients in hopes of creating the perfect drug.

Have you ever wondered why the most common side effects of pharmaceutical products are geared toward making you want to lie down? Nausea, headaches, drowsiness, and dizziness. All of these attack either your stomach or your head. If you were to eat or drink something rotten or spoiled, your stomach would react, letting you know that this substance is not good for you. That whatever you just put inside of you is now at odds with the perfect function of your anatomy. This is the nausea, and it occurs as a natural alarm system.

But like any good burglar, they have to try and combat your alarm system. They do this by throwing you off balance, affecting your equilibrium. This is the dizziness; it's done in an attempt to distract you, forcing you to lend more focus and attention to the otherwise menial task of maintaining your harmony of movement and stability, and less on what's really wrong with you. But none of that would be possible without adequately affecting the brain. Because even the dizziness could be overcome with enough sharpness of focus and attention. Enter in the headaches. Anytime the brain suffers any sort of irregularities, even something as simple as a lack of water, you experience what's known as a headache.

This means that there is something taking effect in your brain. Disrupting the sharpness of your focus. These people are developing drugs that intentionally poke and prod around in your head.

A headache can become so distracting and so totally consuming of our thoughts that you would rather stay in bed on the night of your prom than go out for this once-in-a-lifetime opportunity. You would rather lie there with a pillow over your head than get up and go into work. You would rather miss the finals for your midterms than go at it with a piercing headache.

Now add in all of those other symptoms, and what have you become? Putty in the hands of the person who first mixed all of those ingredients together to begin with. WITCHCRAFT, or, as you call it, pharmacy.

But what would they have to gain by intentionally putting forth drugs with side effects that make you want nothing more out of life than a nice comfy bed and a fluffy pillow? Let's unpack that idea... If you missed your prom, you'd probably become depressed. If you miss too much work, you'll probably get fired. If you fail to pass your exams, you'll probably fail to graduate. What do all of these have in common?

A compromising and vulnerable position. They want you to be vulnerable. A vulnerable person is thirty times more likely to develop an addiction than someone who is secure in their life. And since life is full of cause and effect, allow me to lay out the path before you. Once you are placed in a compromising and vulnerable position, and have turned to drugs as your solution, then as a result of that have become an addict, you are now nearly seventy times more likely to engage in criminal activity. So, to answer your question, what do they have to gain? You becoming an addict and developing into a criminal. That's what they have to gain.

These drugs are created with a vicious and demonic intent. They create them just so that you will become physically dependent. They create them just so that once you're hooked, you'll do anything to get them. They create them just so that while you're on them you'll have all sorts of criminal thoughts.

In my opinion: the pharmaceutical companies, the drug cartel, the police force, the judicial system, and the prisons are all in cahoots. It's one big racquet.

I do want to go on record here and state that though not all police are under their direct payroll, neither the judicial workers nor the prison employees, they are all directly linked together intricately and systematically. In fact the dependency one has on the other is crucial to each one's survival, from a financial standpoint.

If you were to get searched by a cop and they found a bottle of prescription pain pills on you, without a prescription, it would be a crime. Putting it another way, if you had the product without a proper receipt, it would be a crime. But wait a minute, if pharmaceutical companies are structured just like any other business out there, why, all of a sudden, are there laws enforcing their products and not others? And why do you think that is?

Maybe because pain pills are dangerous and can kill you, and they have to know that you are qualified…? Something similar to the laws concerning guns, right? You would think, but not quite.

If your safety were their concern, then following that logic, a person couldn't be in possession of a chainsaw without proof of purchase. Neither would you be able to own any power tool, bottle of bleach, gasoline, a chef's knife, or anything else for that matter that could become lethal, without proof of purchase from the maker or an authorized retailer. In fact, all independent sellers of products that fall into the "hazardous" category would be illegal—online, garage sales, etc., they'd all be banned. With that being said it's safe to say that your safety is not their focus, nor is it their concern.

It's all about money.

My time in prison has allowed me a very close look at how gangs work and operate. And what I've come to notice is that the pharmaceutical companies operate in the same manner. It's called extortion.

So let's go back to the situation where you were found with the bottle of pills. If you have a pass from the gangsters, you're good to go. That means you've paid your extortion fee and there won't be any consequences. But if you've obtained those pills from another source and they didn't get their cut, you're in for it. Their muscle (cops) are going to ruff you up (courts) and make you pay ten times more than what you owe (prison).

It's also not a crime for me to sell the drug, either, as long as I have paid all my dues to the gangsters. And they get their cut. If I got caught outside of a drug store selling a pain pill to someone, I'd be going away for a long time. But it's perfectly legal to sell them if I've paid my college tuition, earned the title of pharm tech, and are employed by the company. We're all good, as long as you kick the profits back up the chain of command. But you, the little guy, a private vendor. Not at all.

You see, it's not the act itself that they deem to be a crime, it's who gets the money. If the money doesn't circulate within this particular gang, then they'll take you out of the game. (And please, do not misunderstand this as an argument to be able to do or sell pharmaceutical drugs without repercussions from the law. What I am making the argument for is the criminality of phar-maceutical pain meds as a whole.)

Did you know that the United States is responsible for 20 percent of the world's incarcerated population? In fact the US has a total prison population of 2 million. The closest nation in prison population is China, with 1.7 million. But the biggest difference lies in the total population of those two nations. America has 332 million. Whereas China has over a billion more people, with a total population of 1.4 billion. So how is it that the US has such a large portion of its population incarcerated in prison?

Drugs.

During my many years inside the prison system, I've had the exclusive opportunity to speak with hundreds of inmates over the years. And do you know what the common thread is between them all? You guessed it, drugs.

Drugs are at the root of nearly 85 percent of all crimes committed in the US. Let's just start with some easily researchable stats. 16.8 percent of all crimes are property. 14.4 consist purely of drug charges, and 12.4 are of the public disorderly, drunk driving, and probation violation type. That alone makes up for 44 percent of all crimes committed. And the exclusive privilege of conversing with convicted prisoners has given me the understanding that nearly 98 percent of all those convicted of property crimes, drug use was at the root of it.

Now as for the murderers and violent offenders. At least half of the guys in here for these types of offenses have attributed their crime to the fact that drugs were involved. Just like with the property group, they were either high when they did it, trying to get high, or someone high pushed them into a situation where it ended in violence or death.

If you were to take drugs out of the equation, the US prison population would look something like this... 588,000, instead of this... 2,153,600.

The establishment of prison is often referred to as either a machine, a warehouse, or an assembly line, pick your poison. In this, people are the product or the commodity that this machine produces or that this warehouse holds in storage or that are shuffled along the conveyor belt. And the drugs are the oil which greases the wheels or keeps the lights on. Without drugs, this machine would go from a raging steam engine train, barreling down the track, to a slow and sluggish cart ride down the path at your local zoo.

Here's another example of how the drugs themselves are not what the system considers a crime but rather the crime lies in who makes the money.

(The following is in regard to the Florida prisons.) Once an individual is in prison, and you have become a financial security for the state, if you were to get caught with any number of drugs, whether it be felonious or not, the punishment for this would be different than if you were free. In fact the distance between the two standards of punishment is so vast that it's insulting. For instance, an ounce of cocaine on the street, depending on the county, would land you a minimum of fifteen years. Get caught with that same ounce inside the prison, sixty days in a cell.

The product is still the same, the act is still the same. So you have to ask yourself, what is the difference? A fenced-in border? Is it the uniform you now wear? Is it the inmate number they assigned to you? Yes, yes, and yes.

While you are in prison, you are worth (hypothetically) a minimum of 140 dollars per day. That's $51,100 a year. Factor in any free labor you do, you're probably worth $60,000 a year. The overhead is dirt cheap, literally next to nothing. A meal comes to about seventeen cents per inmate. At that rate, you could feed a thousand inmates each day, with only two individual inmates per diem. That leaves pure profit on 998 other inmates. The water and electric are given a severely discounted rate. Clothing and hygiene are almost nonexistent. The hygiene provided consists of one bar of hotel soap and a roll of toilet paper a week. Anything else you must buy it yourself.

Clothes are recycled from one inmate to the next, year after year, until they're nothing but holey rags. Bedding and linen are more of the same. Health care is a joke. It seems as though once you enter into prison, ibuprofen is the only remedy needed. High blood pressure, ibuprofen; sun burn, ibuprofen; you fell and dislocated your hip, ibuprofen.

People have now become a commodity. The more people they have in custody the more money they're granted from the federal government. And now that you're their property and making THEM a sufficient amount of money, it's not as bad that you have, use, or sell this same product that got you the ten years to begin with.

This alone screams just how much the system not only doesn't care that you're ruining your life and the lives around you, but that it can kill you. Its only care and concern are who makes the money.

This is a game of treachery and trickery. That's all it is. And we addicts are the pawns that get pushed around with little to no regard or value. We are the ones that the rich use to fluff their pillows and to tip their waitresses. Our misery and our affliction are what they bank on to send their great-great-great grandkids to the best colleges and to make sure that their cars drive themselves and that their homes are so large that an intercom is needed to beckon their maid's butlers.

It's us, we are the ones who support their luxury. While you sell and trade your body for the next hit, they're selling and trading stocks, preparing for the next century. While you visit your loved one in prison or at the graveyard, they visit their loved ones on yachts and in private jets.

And if that wasn't enough to convince you that this was all done by design, I want you to think back to the first time you were introduced to this thing called drugs. Was it in your twenties? Your teens? I'm willing to bet that the first time you were introduced to drugs was somewhere in your elementary school years. When I was growing up, the program they used to try and "raise awareness" about drugs was called the DARE program. They raised awareness all right.

Why is it that the first time I'm introduced to this thing called drugs, it's coming from the very people who are going to one day enforce and regulate the drugs? Happenstance? Not in the least bit. Again, this was done by design. The whole operation was methodically crafted so that the results would be nothing short of what we've already discussed: a nation of crime-committing addicts.

Basic psychology will tell you that if you show a child, especially one from the ages of seven to ten, something new and tell them that they can't have it, it will only strengthen their resolve to obtain that thing.

Seriously, think about it... "This is called a drug. It will make you see and feel stuff that is really cool, and everyone will want to be your friend...but don't believe them. It's all lies, and this thing called a drug is not good for you."

I know all too well that, as a child, I had to experience everything for myself. There was no other way I was going to believe you. Tell me the stove was hot, I had to touch it. You tell me not to play with the socket, I had to stick my finger in it. The only thing they accomplished was making certain that at the earliest convenience I'm going to try this thing called drugs. Thank you, DARE program.

If that's not enough, just look at the acronym they chose for it. DARE.

Have you ever dared a kid to do anything or not to do something? Again, this is simple psychology. Something that's so easily observed using common sense. And you mean to tell me that these huge organizations that have all of these agencies working together—police, drug taskforce, child services, etc.— have missed this one simple aspect?

Not at all. This was all done by design. A cruel and evil design.

Now that you know this. Now that you are inexcusable, and you have no room to say that you were ignorant of the facts, what do you do? Do you still go out and buy that pill? Do you still go out and sell their product for them? If so, then you are a fool. If you can go out and continue to support this evil, what you're saying is that you are for the side of wrong and not for what's right. You are for the side of manipulation and oppression and not for truth and freedom. You are for the side of evil and not for good, you are for Satan and not for God.

Chapter 11
SOBRIETY, AT LAST

You may have been asking yourself, how did this guy get from being an all-out addict to the person he is today? He's told me about why I have insecurities, the difference between fear and sound mind. He showed me different tactics I use on a daily basis, things that I was doing that I had no idea about and wasn't even aware of. Things like always wanting to experience a win in every situation, and selectively remembering the good times, while conveniently forgetting the bad. But what changed him?

He says it was God, but how does he know that it was God? Have no fear, I haven't brought you this far only to leave you by yourself at the edge. We're going to climb down together.

DECEMBER 2020, Okeechobee, FL

John, that was the guy's name, but at the time, I couldn't remember it. Heck, I barely even recognized him. In fact we'd been neighbors for two months before the notion had ever even hit me. This was him. This was the guy from five years ago who wanted to kill that little girl and her mom.

Somehow, out of the seventy-plus prisons across the state of Florida, and out of the eight different dorms on this particular compound, and out of the three separate wings in this dorm, and from the forty-two other rooms he could have landed in, he was here, right next door. My neighbor.

God was at work.

Neither of us realized who the other was at first. But when we did, it was so very awkward. It's a funny thing. I suspected that he might try something, some form of revenge, but I guess since I didn't tell on him out of a malicious or selfish ambition, I didn't really feel as though I was in very much danger at all. I was still under the belief that if I do good things, I'll get good rewards. As if God operated on the same primitive and loveless rewards-based system as humans do.

At this time, I was a heavy drug addict. Snorting, eating, and drinking molly on a daily basis. When I got too high and hadn't been to sleep in a few days, I would smoke tunechi to calm myself. It's a form of K2, but the prison version, meaning there's no telling what sort of chemicals I was smoking. Then, I'd use Suboxin to finally knock me out and get some sleep. When I woke up, I'd do it all over again.

Needless to say I wasn't very well centered. I hadn't been exercising anymore. My reading of the Word stopped, and my thoughts were fully consumed with getting high.

This guy comes into my room one night, and he's got some molly. My favorite.

"Let me get a bump," I ask him. We worked it out so that when I received my sack I was buying in a few minutes, I'd return the favor... Well, as they say in prison, the only thing you can be certain of is uncertainties. So as it happened, it's the next day, and I'm walking past his room.

"Hey, cracker. Where's my dope?" he calls out.

I stepped into his room explaining how I'd gotten the molly real late and that all of the doors were locked. I couldn't get it to him. And that I'd have to catch him on the next round. Now, mind you, the cost of the bump he gave me might have come up to a dollar. That was it. One dollar's worth of a snort. Pissed me off more than anything, nothing worse than a tease.

"Tighten me up, then," he said. Meaning, *let's fight.*

I shrugged and met him in the back corner. On my way to the grid (what we call the area where we fight), I dropped off the knife I was carrying in my own room. I was not going to need it, right? It's just a fight, I didn't want it to get out of hand.

I'm standing there with my hands up, ready to go, and he's the one who pulls out a knife. Long story short, I get stabbed eleven times. Hand, face, and the top of my head. This was a whole lot more serious than a dollar's worth of molly; I just couldn't see it yet.

As I'm in my room getting bandaged up and after lying down resting for a few days, it finally dawned on me, I didn't get stabbed over a bump of molly, this guy was taking out a hit on me.

God was at work.

Let me explain something to you. The knife was at least six inches long, and at least three times it was buried to the hilt, once in my temple, once in my head, and the last just under my eye. Still got the scars to prove it. And all glory to God, I still have perfect eyesight. By all clinical and logical means, I should be dead, or at least have suffered some sort of brain damage, decreased motor functions, anything. It's nothing short of an act of God as to why I'm here today.

The first day that I was able to move around, I was walking up the stairs to go talk with someone, and I happened to look, and there he was, the guy who stabbed me and tried to take my life. We were eye to eye, staring at each other. The spirit spoke to me in that moment.

I stopped in front of the door and said, "I don't hold anything in my heart against you."

The look on his face was a strange mixture of relief and confusion. He was probably expecting me to retaliate. To wait for just the right moment. Why else would I not go to medical and request protective custody? But no, that wasn't the case, God had other plans.

"Why would you say that?" he asked me.

"That's just what the spirit told me to do." A weight was lifted. It was what we both needed.

I learned about forgiveness that day. I learned that without forgiveness, there can be no love. When un-forgivingness is present, when we are holding on to something that is centered on hate, and centered around selfishness, love cannot enter.

The opposite of love is selfishness, we have to be willing to let go of ourselves. We have to be willing to kill the ego inside of us in order for God to live inside of us.

I'll say it again: the ego must move out, so God can move in...

Deuteronomy 8:2–3: "You shall remember that the LORD your God led you all the way these forty years in the wilderness to humble you and to test you, to know what was in your heart, whether you would keep His commandments or not. So He humbled you, allowed you to hunger, and fed you with manna, which your fathers did not know, nor did you know, that He might make you to know that man does not live by bread alone, but by every word that proceed out from the mouth of the LORD."

That word, "manna," is a Hebrew word which means "what." While you were wondering around this wilderness called life, God fed you with questions. Think about that. If you knew everything, if you were able to go through this life all on your own, then what would you need a question for? The questions you've had throughout life are what He used to humble you. It's what God used to break down your ego, to show you that you don't know everything. And He did it so that His word could enter in.

And since God is love, and love is endless, there was still more that God had in store. There was something bigger he wanted me to see. And believe it or not, I was still getting high. I was still trying to ease my pain and coax all of the emotions I was experiencing with drugs. I was in an all-out battle; my spirit was trying to come alive and speak to me, but my flesh wanted to silence the spirit by staying medicated.

About a week and a half later, John put out another hit on me. This one for even more money. It's not a secret, either. Everyone in the dorm knew what was going on. They were basically licking their lips, just waiting for the right moment to strike. He played the victim all the way out, telling everyone how I snitched on him, but conveniently leaving out that not only did I not get any special relief in my case but that I stopped him from killing a nine-year-old little girl. But I didn't say anything, either. For some reason, I was contempt with allowing whatever was going to happen to me happen.

I would deal with it on my own. I got through it the first time and I'll get through it this time.

But what I failed to realize was that I wasn't the one who got me through anything. God did it. In fact, the drugs were the one trying to kill me by keeping me in the flesh and ignoring the spirit. Man was just the vessel used to take me out.

God was the one at work.

In Genesis 50:20 it says: "...But as for you, you meant evil against me but God meant it for good, in order to bring it about as it is this day, to save many people alive."

God will always use the efforts of the enemy to perform his own agenda. Not saying that God doesn't use his own efforts, but it's always a victory when the enemy thinks he's doing something to destroy or kill you, and in fact, it's being turned the other way. Instead of destruction, you're being restored, and instead of death, you're gaining life. It's one of God's ways of showing His might and His glory. That no matter how hard you try, God will always be triumphant.

Just look at Jesus. Do you think for one second He didn't know who and what Judas was? That Judas would betray Him? But what the enemy meant for evil, God meant for good.

And before I go on with the story, I want to set the stage with this verse... Psalms 55:12–14 (I would encourage you to read the chapter in its entirety): "...For it is not an enemy who reproaches me: Then I could bear it. Nor is it one who hates me, who has exalted himself against me, then I could hide from him. But it was my equal, my companion and my acquaintance. We took sweet council together, and walked to the house of God in the throng."

I go on lockdown for count time in a room with a guy whom I thought to be a friend, though at the time I didn't know it. As it turned out, he was trying to collect on the bounty. But not just any friend, this was a guy who fed me while I was recovering from the first attack and even helped with the bandages. This was a guy whom I shared long discussions about God with. He was also an addict, just like me.

If any of you have ever experienced betrayal, pay attention: As long as we give money the power to control our lives, things like friendship and trust cannot compete. Money buys people's morals.

I can't tell you what did or didn't go through his head, but he never took action. I knew his intentions; he was telegraphing his movements the whole time. He had a knife, I had a knife. We were in a standoff.

I like to believe God intervened. Because as much as I seen him psych himself up to do it, he couldn't. No blood was spilled that day. Thank God.

As soon as the door opened, I went and found the dorm preacher. Every dorm has at least one, a guy who doesn't get involved with any of the foolishness. I told him everything. Every single detail, and I cried while I did it. Then he cried, and I asked him, "Can you baptize me? I want to give my life to God. I'm tired of living like this." He nodded yes. Then we went straight upstairs to his cell, and that's the day I gave my life over to Christ. Right there in a prison cell, God cared enough to show me how much He loves me and how much I need him. I haven't touched a single drug since.

Is that to say that you will have to go through something as traumatic and scary as that in order to get off the drugs...? I don't know. But I can tell you this that no matter what happens in our life, when God wants to pluck you out of the mess, there's nothing that can stop Him. Our responsibility is to respond when He calls us.

If you think that God is calling you, even for just a second. If you even had the slightest fleeting thought imaginable, that is God Almighty Himself calling you. Answer Him, and I promise you He will make everything you're going through, all of your humongous problems, seem so very small.

"But you don't understand, I've done too much bad in my life, God can't save me."

Romans 5:20 says otherwise: "...but where sin abounded, grace abounded much more."

"But you still don't get it, I've denied him hundreds of times and even cursed his name."

You can take every wrong you've ever done and ever thought of doing, or ever will do, yours, the neighbors, and every prisoner in every prison around the world, add it all up, and the verse still says, "...grace abounded MUCH more."

It's as if you worked as a hole digger. You're covered in dirt. You can't relax until you get in the shower and wash it off. Once you do, and you're feeling clean again, you're finally able to move on with your day, kick your feet up on the couch, go out with friends, whatever.

The point is, the little dirt you had on you no longer affects you. It's the same way as when God makes you to go through something. Sure, it feels disgusting for the time being, but when you come out on the other side, none of that even matters anymore.

When God makes you into a new man, the old one is nothing more than a memory, an example of who you used to be and a reminder of just how far you've come. Jesus is waiting to save you.

If you don't understand how the whole Jesus thing works, you're not alone. I didn't get it for a good while either. So here's how it works:

Since God is just and righteous, and there are no falsehoods in Him. And since He is pure truth, a debt must always be paid. If someone owes something, it's only right that it gets paid. Would you go so far as to say that you are in debt? Have you ever wronged anyone in your life? God loves that person just as much as He loves you. And in the same way that your wrongs will be righted, you can expect that for the next person as well. All things must come to perfection if they are to be reunited with God.

Do you see how the things we've done in our life are in opposition to a God that accepts nothing less than perfection? If so, you're on the right track. And this is where Jesus comes in the picture. Stay with me and it will all come together for you.

Let's say that there is a disease taking hold of the world, and it will eventually kill every single human on the planet. But a cure has been discovered. That cure can only be found in the blood of a ten-year-old boy who is the first and only child. Furthermore, it has to be from your specific DNA.

You just so happen to have a son, a ten-year-old son, your only son. He's the sweetest kid ever. Never lies, respects his parents, has love for people and animals, gives away everything he has to kids who don't have. And the government knocks on your door. Says that in order to save the world, your son has to die. You look at that sweet little boy, and you make the hardest decision in the history of the world. You agree.

He asks, "Daddy, what's going on?"

"You're going to save the world, son," you say to him, and he smiles. You take him with you to the lab, and stand by idly as you watch them drain him of every ounce of precious blood he has in his body.

This is what God did for the world. His endless love was poured out on us through the sacrifice of his only begotten son. But He wanted more than just to save us from our disease of sin, God wanted to experience eternity with us. He wanted us to experience eternity with Him. So how did God do that? By defeating not only the disease of sin, but by defeating death.

Jesus Christ conquered not only the world and every power and dominion on this planet, but He even conquered death. Jesus had in his possession all of the love that the Father had, and with that, He descended into hell, took back the keys to the everlasting separation from God that we were doomed to experience, and then ascended, to sit at the right hand of God. And right now, as you read these words, He's there, saying to God, "I died for this one also. Their debt is paid in full."

And now comes the part where you start to be fed with the manna. "I think I might need to be saved? Will he save me? Did he die for me also?" This is probably the most common, and most humbling, question people start asking. It shows that you realize just how broken and helpless you truly are.

Psalms 34:18: "...The LORD is near to those who have a broken heart, and saves such as have a contrite spirit."

"And what do I have to do to be saved?" Let's see what the apostle Paul says, Romans 10:9: "...confess with your mouth the Lord Jesus and believe in your heart that God has raised Him from the dead, you will be saved."

It's that simple. God loves the world so much that He canceled out all of our work and efforts of qualifying for everlasting life and cast the entire responsibility upon the cross. And now, "whosoever believes in Him will not perish, but have everlasting life," John 3:16.

And how does that work? How can one person's sacrifice be sufficient enough for the entire world?

It's in the blood. The precious blood that Jesus spilled on that cross contains in it, all of the righteousness of heaven. So once we accept Jesus for who He is, the Son of God, and he awakens your spirit, He begins to live inside of you. Now, when God looks down from Heaven at you, all he sees is His Son.

PART TWO...The Family
CHAPTER 12

This portion is dedicated to those who were impacted by my addiction the most. My family. As well as family members of other addicts. The dilemma of addiction is so multi-faceted that it cannot be covered from a single perspective.

In the following chapters you will experience some of the raw emotion that the addict inflicts upon their loved ones. This section exists for two reasons. The first is for the addict. Perhaps they have never stopped and taken an honest look at the way they affect those closest to them. Perhaps it's never truly registered. I can only hope that if nothing else, it will make you want to stop using, and see just how much of a negative impact you've had on those who love you will do the trick.

And the second reason is for the families themselves. Your struggle is not an isolated event. There are mothers, fathers, and siblings all over who are experiencing the exact same things. Does this take away any of the situations' significance? Absolutely not. It reinforces it. This section was written with the hope that you, the person who deeply loves their son or daughter or sister or brother, and is tired of seeing them struggle in their addiction, may find some solace. That you might discover a way to reach that person. That it might help you in any way.

The first person you are about to meet has a master's in social work and psychology. There's an ongoing joke that she only entered that field because of the broken relationships in her own home growing up (we're blessed to have the sort of relationship that allows us to talk about things openly without shame). She's someone very dear to me. Her name is Amanda, and she is my sister.

CHAPTER 13

I can still remember the first time I saw my brother freaking out, due to being high. It wasn't even eight in the morning. I didn't have class that day, so I thought I would sleep in. All I could hear was slamming doors and my brother yelling.

I got up and looked out my bedroom window to see my brother frantically searching the ground in the backyard while yelling at the dogs to get away. I went out to the living room to try to record his actions. I opened the door to ask what was wrong and what he was looking for. He saw my iPod and started to curse at me for recording him and kept asking, "Where is it? Where did he put it?"

I didn't understand and asked what he was talking about. He became angrier and told me to stop acting dumb and trying to cover for him. I told him again I didn't know what he was talking about.

"My weed! Where the fuck is it? Where did he hide it?"

"What? Where did who hide it?"

"Your dad! I know he hid it! He's always doing this shit! They're always messing with me and acting like it's a big deal. It's just weed!"

"Jeremy, no one is hiding anything. Maybe you just misplaced it."

He continued to yell and rant about my dad hiding his weed. He looked like a madman while he searched. His eyes were wide and had a frantic look to them. His clothes and hair were disheveled, as if he hadn't slept or showered in days even though he just woke up and was getting ready to go to work. He was sweating and had that musty sweat smell to him. He searched the house for another twenty minutes or so and then everything became quiet. I went out to see what happened, and he was like a totally different person. He was chipper and informed me he was going to work now. I asked about his weed; he said he found it. It was in his room the whole time. When he said where he found it, he had a sheepish grin and chuckled before leaving.

He never apologized, he just left with his little bag of weed. I don't know what he was on, but I never seen him act that way before and never forgot. He always insisted he wasn't addicted but he smoked weed as much and as often as a chain smoker smoked cigarettes. One when he woke up, one with coffee or breakfast, one on the way to work, one at work, one on the drive to the next site, one at the job site, one with lunch, one on the way home, one after dinner, and one before bed. It got to a point where I couldn't remember the last time I saw him without bloodshot eyes.

I started noticing bloody tissues in my bathroom trash can. I knew it was more than weed, but couldn't bring myself to say anything to him. He was gone for four years and just came back home and didn't want him to get mad at me and leave again. I even went as far as printing out a Christmas package form and was going to give it to him to fill it out, because I didn't think he would make it to Christmas that year. I chickened out and threw it away. That's one thing I've always regretted, because one month later he was back in jail awaiting trial.

I don't think he'll ever truly understand the impact his drug use has had on me and my life. I'm sure this goes the same for most of the family members of drug addicts. Drugs can make even the most selfless person selfish. All they can think about is that next high. How can I get it? When can I do it?

I'm not sure why people do drugs. According to my studies, many people turn to drugs due to past traumas, whether it's emotional or physical. Most use drugs/alcohol to self-medicate. To help numb any pain they may have and make life more bearable. I believe most people get addicted to the feeling a drug gives them more than the actual drug itself.

But what I want you to know, more than anything, is that I don't know the WHY. And it's frustrating. And it's confusing. It makes you question yourself and if there was anything you've done wrong. And in the end, you'll never know why. Not unless they come to sobriety, and are willing to open up like my brother did.

Growing up with an addict is horrible.

By: Amanda, sister of an addict

Wow! I was completely blind sighted when I first came to realize that my son was using drugs.

I first noticed some changes in his attitude just after middle school, and I just figured it was because we had just made a move from Puerto Rico to Florida. You know the thing pre-teens and teenagers hate the most is a new school and having to make new friends all over again. I went to the school and had a talk with the guidance counselor, and of course, what did she say... ? Don't worry, it's puberty, it's harder for boys to adjust than girls. I wasn't buying it. I knew something else was going on, but at the time I was not sure what it was.

I, like most parents, was in denial. I kept thinking could he be doing drugs... No, there's no way he's using drugs,. Then I would think where would he get them from and how would he even know how to make a drug deal. We don't live in that kind of neighborhood. So it turns out it doesn't matter where you live: drugs are everywhere, even in the most unsuspecting places.

I was devastated when I realized what was going on with him, and I'm sure, like many other mothers whose children use drugs, I thought, *This is all my fault*. How could I have let this happen to my son? What did I do wrong? How can I fix this? I had no idea what we were up against... This was not something you could just fix.

We tried picking who his friends should or shouldn't be, punishment, counseling, moving from one neighborhood to another, even moved to a different state hoping that would help... It didn't.

I'd ask him over and over again why he felt the need to do drugs, and he always had the same answer, "I don't know why. I just like it, that's all!" I'd ask him to help me to understand what he was going through and if there was anything we as a family could do to change, to help him get through whatever he was going through so he wouldn't feel the need to get high. His response: "I'm not going through anything, I just like it!"

That right there told me I knew absolutely nothing about addictions. And it just broke my heart to see my only son living in a constant fog. All my hopes and dreams for him had been stolen from him because of drugs and how this would follow him the rest of his life.

As a baby, I always promised to protect him from all harm and to always take care of him, and to not let anything create the kind of childhood I had grown up with. I failed!

If you have never had a child or a loved one addicted to drugs, you will not understand the pain and anguish this causes one to go through. You just want to make it stop but you don't know how; everything you try does not work. You go through a lot of phases, denial, anger, compassion, fear, anger, confusion, hurt, dismay, embarrassment, sadness, the blame game, and, again, anger.

You blame everyone for their drug addiction but the drug addict, I know I did. It was the girlfriend's fault, or it was those kids he's been hanging out with, the drug dealer, then it's the drug company's fault. And depending on what type of drugs they are on, to some extent, it is the drug companies that have played a part in their addiction, since they know how additive their drugs are, and yet they keep making them, and we all know why....

I myself and my family have been robbed by his drug addiction. I have many memories of family vacations, camping trips, weekend cookouts, and holiday gatherings. But when I recall those memories, someone is always missing: it's my son. He would always refuse to do these family things, and if forced to come along, he would make life miserable for everyone or just wonder off on his own and not join in on whatever the plan was for the day.

I think his sister had it the worst. Keep in mind there is a seven-year age difference between the two of them and he is the oldest. Therefore, he didn't want her tagging along with him or around him when his friends came over to the house; he would always push her aside. He was never there for any of her milestones as she was growing up—the transition to middle school (I sent him away to a boot-camp so that he could graduate high school), high school prom or graduation (he was in prison). He made it home just in time for her twenty-first Birthday. She was so happy that he was there to share that day with her. College, he missed her college years and graduation, also missed her graduation, when she got her master's degree. (He was in prison again.)

All these years that they as brother and sister were robbed...because of the drugs. And sadly, but truthfully, she was placed on the back burner by myself and her father because we were always so worried about her brother. Never once did I worry about her. She was the child who did all the right things, never got in trouble, always an honor student with very good grades, never complained when she could not have certain things because the money was going towards counseling for her brother.

Here I thought she had it all together. Again, I was wrong! Don't get me wrong, she's a very smart, strong, and independent woman now. Today she is twenty-seven years old and is seeing a counselor for the many things that went wrong in her childhood, things that I did not notice. I had no idea how his drug use and behavior affected her. All she ever wanted was to be close to her brother, but he either pushed her away or the drugs pulled him away. Either way, her childhood was robbed from her, having to deal with such big issues that she did not understand as a little girl.

This portion of the book was to explain how my son's drug use made me feel at the time we were struggling to get him off the drugs. The strange thing is, I cannot recall those exact feelings/emotions. All I know is that there is, finally, after all these years, a light at the end of the tunnel. It's only by the Grace of God that my son has finally found his way back home.

In the past year to two years, I am seeing the son I had before the drugs took hold of him, and now the only feelings I can say without a doubt are thankfulness and praises to God.

I had always prayed for God to make him stop using drugs. One day I realized I was praying for the wrong thing. It occurred to me that all that time I should have been asking God to help him find a way to find God and to open up his heart to Him. And low and behold that's what happened.

Of course, it was done in God's special and unexplainable way. But nonetheless, my son realized he needed God in order to get off the drugs, as he has pretty much stated throughout this book. If it had not been for the Grace of God, you would not be reading this book. Let all the glory be to God!

I respectfully implore anyone who reads this book to please pass it along to friends and loved ones, so that they may find some understanding of what an addict is dealing with.

Don't give up on an addict, there is always hope, even when you can't see it!

By: Karen, mother of an addict

In 2019, about twenty million people in the United States had a substance use disorder in the past year, according to the most recent data report. Read that again. Twenty million people. I am the wife of an addict. Addiction affects more than just the addict. It affects everyone who loves them and everyone around them. The statistics about addicts are staggering. You can read more here: https://www.addictionresource.net/2021-addiction-statistics/.

How addiction affected me

I have never been addicted to a drug. However, I did drink too much in my younger years, but I've never been an addict. With that being said, I have been severely affected by drug addiction. I can't tell you exactly what the addict goes through when they are in active addiction. But what I can tell you is how it affected me, the wife of an addict.

I can't even begin to tell you how many times I've felt betrayed. Every time my husband lied to me, it was as if he was choosing the drug over our relationship. It was as if he couldn't care less whether or not the lie would put a rift in our relationship.

Addicts will lie to get what they want. They will manipulate you to meet their needs, regardless of what it costs you. A lot of the times I knew he was lying, but was so afraid that if I called him on it, he'd leave me. I knew that he was so volatile that the slightest offense could send him on a tail spin. So I was forced to stand there and be lied to right in my face, time and again. Damned if you do, damned if you don't sort of thing.

Next on my list of severely endured wounds, feeling abandoned. Our life was no longer "Our life." It was all about him. I was left on the outside looking in. I felt as though our marriage was a moving car. And my husband was driving, while I tried to hold on to the bike rack on the roof.

I knew none of his plans. And when I did come up with any plans and would discuss it with him, a day later it was as if amnesia had crept in; he remembered none of it.

A certain numbness comes along with being an addict. And that's mainly because addicts can only see their next fix; it separates them emotionally from the world around them. They become incapable of caring about you or anything else.

This drove my anxiety levels through the roof. I suffered panic attacks, loss of sleep. I didn't want to eat, and felt afraid— constantly felt afraid. For myself, and for him. When life is uncertain, fear is always close by. Just read through the Bible. Nearly every time God tells us to "Fear not,", He almost immediately reminds us of just how secure and infallible His promises are.

Setting boundaries

Setting boundaries is one of the most important and difficult things to do when dealing with an addict. I had to set very clear boundaries. Setting boundaries, while an addict is in active addiction, is more for self-preservation than for anything.

The addict will not and cannot respect those boundaries. And how can we expect them to? They won't even respect their own. Those boundaries are to protect yourself, your mental health, and your finances. You have to decide where to draw the line. How far you are willing to go down that path. How much you want to enable them. Once they are in recovery, new boundaries need to be set. Clear and firm boundaries.

Expectations. This will set you up for more heartache and pain than we deserve. A lot of times we place expectations on the addict that are just plain unreasonable. And as soon as the addict cannot meet those expectations, we get upset. So if you find yourself continually being let down, it's probably due to unreasonable expectations.

You cannot save them

This is the most difficult thing to accept and understand: you cannot save them. You cannot. In fact, you must let their hand go. They have to fall. They have to hit the bottom. This is the hardest part of dealing with active addiction. Watching them fall. Until an addict hits rock bottom, they will not be ready to recover. Even after hitting rock bottom, it may take several tries to get and stay sober.

Don't get me wrong, I've had to check my own expectations in this area. And it's not a battle that I can even fully understand yet, from their point of view, that is. I do know how hard it was to watch my husband fall. To feel like I had to protect myself from him. I read a quote once that stayed with me. It said, "If an addict is happy with you, you are probably enabling them. If an addict is angry at you, you're probably trying to save their life." That is the truest thing I have read.

Recovery is hard

Truth is, it won't always be a happy ending. That's a hard reality. You can love someone and not enable them (that entails telling them NO). You can pray for someone from a distance and still keep your mental health intact.

If you're anything like me, and love way too hard, the next thing I'm about to tell you will resonate deeply. Do your best to try and keep yourself as the priority. As hard as it may be, DO NOT give in. Let them know through your actions, not just words, that there are actual consequences to their actions.

When they are ready to make a change, they will let you know. Until then, put one foot in front of the other, take one minute at a time, and find support. With twenty million addicts in this country, you won't have to go far to find someone affected.

Recovery is difficult for the addict, as well as for the people they affected. It's a lot of work to rebuild what was broken. Things will not go back to being the same, either. It will be a life adjustment for both the addict and the loved one.

Trust has been broken, feelings have been hurt, and relationships have to be built from the ground up. You both have to want it and be willing to work towards it. Trust takes a lot of time to build, and can be destroyed in a day. Patience is a key part of rebuilding. It's important to discuss how things affected you, so you can let it go. Holding onto things and bringing them back up over and over is not healthy. Talk about it, let it hurt, and then let it go. We are nineteen months sober now, with a lifetime to go.

By: Lori, Wife of an addict

Part Three...

THE PARADOX

Up to this point you've read all about the various things in our lives which drive us to want to use drugs. I'm sure that not every core issue or problem has been identified. But at least the ones that I can do you justice in displaying.

Here's the "so what" chapter. Here is the grand sum of it all. Here is your unbreakable cord.

Everything has two sides. All of creation was brought about in duality. I want to bring you to the first page of the Bible. Genesis, chapter one... "In the beginning God created the heavens and the earth. The earth was void and without form and darkness was over the deep. And the spirit of God hovered over the waters."

Most people just simply gloss over this. You see, at first glance you would just assume that this is nothing more than a prerequisite to the rest of the creation story. But it's not. It's the very first sentence in the Bible for a reason. Your understanding of the entire book is subsequent and hinges on this one statement. So let's examine it.

An earth is an earth because of its form. It is made up of either gas or liquid or solid, but it has a form, it's not void. So why does the Bible say that the earth was void? Did the author not know what those words meant? Void, without form? Perhaps the earth he's speaking about is not a physical one. Perhaps it's not an earth at all... Heaven, in general, is located above. Earth would, in turn, be below. Above and below. Benevolent and malevolent. Good and bad.

The first sentences in the Bible allude to the fact that the very first thing ever created was opposites.

Look at the wording and the punctuation. After it tells you about the earth and how formless and void it is, you find a semicolon. The very next thing you read after telling about the earth is a description of it that "darkness is over the deep." That this "earth" is the below, the deep, and that darkness is over it. And this is said in contrast to the heavens. "And the spirit of God hovered over the waters." Darkness is over the earth, or the deep, and the spirit of God is over the heavens.

If you keep reading, you'll notice a pattern: everything that gets created has its opposite. Light, dark. Earth (as in dirt), water. Grass, seed. Tree, fruit. Bird, fish. Sun, moon. Beast, insect. Man, woman.

In the same chapter at verse twenty-six: "He created the man in His image." That word image in the original Hebrew text means "shade" or "phantom."

Shade: 1. A property that becomes apparent when light falls on an object and by which things that are identical in form can be distinguished. 2. A very small amount.

With this we can see what the writer of Genesis was trying to convey. Us, humans, you and me, we are a property in which God's light touches, and now we have become distinguishable. But only in a very small amount.

Let's give it some application. Imagine you're standing outside and your shadow is being cast out in front of you. You can distinguish whether or not this is a male or a female. How much weight you have, the length of hair. You can more or less come away with a general outline for the shape of the one who cast the shadow.

Except there's a whole lot of information left out. What color shirt are they wearing? Shoes? Are they happy? This is us, the shade. What we so desperately need in this life, in order to ever truly know who we are and where we come from, we need to look back at what is casting the shadow.

If Josh's story hit home with you and your search for your identity, don't miss that last part. But just to be sure let me say it again... What we so desperately need in this life, in order to ever truly know who we are and where we come from, all we need is to look back at Who is the one casting our shadow.

Moving on. After man was made, God rested. That was it. He accomplished what he set out to do. If you've been engineering a building for the last twenty years, your greatest work yet, the day you complete it is the day you can rest.

If you don't believe that we are God's greatest creation, do this: trace a line from the top of your head and bring it down the center, over the length of your body. What do you notice? Complete and perfect symmetry. Two halves to your brain. Two eyes. Two ears, two nostrils. Two tubes in your throat, two lungs, two arms, two valves in your heart, two intestines, two testicles (for the men), two legs, etc.... Only ONE mouth, ONE belly button, ONE sexual organ, ONE anus, and ONE BODY.

I'll get to the singulars in just a moment. But look at how we were made. Our entire composition is based on duality. The things which keep us alive—our brains, our lungs, and our heart—they all operate in a dual nature. The brain has two sides. Male and female. It can both send and receive information. The lungs, a left and right lung, they breathe in and then breathe out. The heart. It performs two operations: pumping blood in and then out. Even our blood has two types of cells, red and white.

The way we perceive and interact with the world is even done in pairs. Our eyes, ears, nose, hands, and feet. When we put anything inside of us, it enters in through the mouth and then gets divided between two tubes, either for air or for food and drink.

At this point you're probably wondering about the singulars that are on our bodies, as well as the body itself. The mouth, the belly button, the sex organ, and the anus. What do each of these have in common, other than being a singular? It's their ability to either create or destroy. So with the singular, comes the ability to create. Whereas the duality can only ever be a creation, to either help sustain creation, or experience the creation.

Let's start with the mouth. Let's see how James so eloquently describes our mouth or, more specifically, our tongue.

"For we all stumble in many things. If anyone does not stumble in word, he is a perfect man, able also to bridle the whole body. Indeed, we put bits in horse's mouths that they may obey us, and we turn their whole body. Look also at ships: although they are so large and are driven by fierce winds, they are turned by a very small rudder wherever the pilot desires. Even so the tongue is a little member and boasts great things.

See how great a forest a little fire kindles! And the tongue is a fire, a world of iniquity. The tongue is so set among our members that it defiles the whole body, and sets on fire the course of nature and it is set on fire by hell. For every kind of beast and bird, of reptiles and creature of the sea, is tamed and has been tamed by mankind. But no man can tame the tongue. It is an unruly evil, full of deadly poison. With it we bless our God and Father, and with it we curse men, who have been made in the similitude of God. Out of the same mouth proceed blessing and cursing." James 3:2–10

With your words, you can either create peace or strife. You can either encourage or discourage. You can build up or tear down. "Life and death are in the power of the tongue."

If you pay attention, you'll start to notice a common theme through the rest of our singularities. The navel, while you were still in the womb, served the purpose of delivering all of your nutrients. These nutrients which entered through your navel could have either destroyed you or given you nourishment. Life or death.

The sex organ, it either brings about life or it passes on disease, and, in the worst cases, death. Lastly, the anus. I know this may be a bit touchy for some, but regardless of your opinion in what is or isn't appropriate, the anus is a part of our body. We were all born with it, and we all use it. This area, as we know, produces fecal matter, and that gross and smelly stuff has two very important functions. It either becomes pure waste and becomes a poison should you reenter it into your system, or it can be used as fertilizer, depending on your diet.

So what? So what the entire universe was made in pairs? So what if we're made in such perfect harmony with nature that our bodies are a direct reflection of all creation? What does any of this mean? What does it have to do with me? Two answers. (Again, pairs.) First, it was laid out so that you can see clearly that you were created with a purpose, on purpose, for a purpose. But secondly, and this is the application of it, the very simple application: We have a responsibility. A responsibility to either follow God or follow Satan. Will we follow God's will and plans for life and create life? Or will we go against what God would have us do and produce death?

What does all of this have to do with the addict? Everything. You were created with the ability to perform two opposing functions. Either good or evil. Your addiction is no different.

The dictionary defines the addict as

1. A person who has become physiologically or psychologically dependent on a habit-forming substance.

2. To occupy or involve oneself habitually or compulsively.

3. A devoted adherent or fan.

Now take a moment to examine what an addict truly is, apart from the use of drugs. An addict is a person who is fully committed and devoted to a thing and is fully involved in it. Determination. That's actually a good quality. The only time being an addict becomes a problem is when we choose to lend that gift of determination over to the enemy. It's a crime that should be regarded on the same level as treason. You take what your president, or captain, or if you're in a gang, your OG, you take the sacred knowledge, tools, and abilities and you use it to promote the enemy.

The level and amount of determination we have was given to us by God Himself. A gift. A superpower even. Think about it. While you were in your addiction, there was nothing that could stop you from accomplishing your goal of getting high. You would overcome such great obstacles, out talk anyone, make something out of nothing, all for your cause. God gave you that ability. We've just been using it for the enemy's purposes this whole time.

Right now, your brain is hard at work. There are thousands if not tens of thousands of synapses firing off and sending signals throughout the rest of your body. Every fractal of light, every smell and sound, the continuous sensation your skin experiences, whether it be the feel of the clothes you're wearing or the temperature of the air around you. Every breath you take, inhale and exhale, filtering in vital oxygen and expelling poisonous carbon monoxide. All of this is done without any effort on your part. Not for a single moment do you have to stop and try to do any of these things. And even more importantly, if you failed to perform any of these simple tasks, it could mean life or death.

Think about it. What if you got hit by an incoming train because you failed to interpret the shape of the object or its velocity and direction it was heading in? What if you couldn't hear it? What if you couldn't decipher the temperature and ended up burning alive or freezing to death? Try to hold your breath as long as you can; in fact, stop breathing all together. You can't. You will instinctively take another breath. Because your very existence depends upon this.

Yes, these are dramatic examples, but I'm making a point. And the point is this: inside of your brain are neural pathways in which this instinctual information travels along, on a continual basis. And try if you will, but you cannot undo any of the hard wiring that has already been laid. It's now part of your nature, it's who you are. It is an unbreakable cord.

Do you see it now?

Drugs, over time, form this same sort of cord. The same way our brain recognizes the importance of these certain thoughts and deems them vital to our survival, the drugs form a cord in our brain that sends the same sort of urgent signal.

Wake up and don't have any dope for the day, or even have an avenue of where or how you're going to get high today. You will instantly focus all of your energy on this one act, on this one goal. You will get the feeling as if the world is going to come to an end and life as you know it will be over. I can't tell you how many times I've used the phrase "I'll die if I don't have any drugs."

That's because your brain has formed a synthesized version of these same unbreakable cords. The same instinctually styled reactions you'd have towards it being too hot or too cold, you try and fix it. The same way if a train was headed towards you, you'd move. It becomes instinct. Your brain sends the signal, and your body reacts.

So, let's look at your unbreakable cord.

The unbreakable cord: if your addiction is likened to a steel cable, so strong that it can't be broken, then that means that with one thread after another, it has been weaved into what it is today. And if it has been weaved together, then that means that another layer can still be added. Then another, and another. Until tomorrow's cord looks nothing like todays. So, in reality, your addiction cord is not yet complete and never will be.

So what are we weaving over this unbreakable cord? Should we continue to put on the same negative and destructive habits? Absolutely not. Whenever your mind starts to push you in the direction of thinking about the drug or getting high, by tricking you into thinking there is a problem, instantly, you need to try and weave something different.

You've already been equipped with enough information and ammunition to know when the enemy is trying to trick you. Keep everything you've learned in the front of your mind, and use it against the enemy.

When your mind starts sending the signal of a problem, whether it be depression, anger, anxiety, stress, or just boredom, and your cord is telling you to continue weaving the drug habit on top of it. When you hear the lie being spoken, that the drug is the thing which will fix your problem. This is the moment in which you react and counter with something positive. And there is no greater power you can possibly use other than the name. Jesus.

Then put on your headphones and listen to music. Drown the voices out. Go for a bike ride or a walk and imagine that you are physically moving away from the temptation. Eat a snack, exercise, anything. But don't stop. Keep doing this. It's not a one-time application. You didn't become a drug addict overnight, so neither will this process happen overnight. And before long, your unbreakable cord of drug addiction and misery will become an unbreakable cord of freedom and happiness.

If you're looking for someone to tell you how to fix an addiction problem, and you don't think that you have to put in any work, you're in for a long ride that will only drop you off at the same spot you got on at. No two people are the same. No two people can work their lives out using the same processes and techniques. That is part of life's beauty, that we all must find our own route to the same destination. Happiness and fulfilment.

All that has been talked about here was in hopes that you might see and know that you're not alone. You are not the only one who has suffered from these things. That I have experienced these very same problems, and even more so, have overcome. That the addiction is not WHO I am. It's what I've done.

Addiction is not WHO you are, it's what you've done.

Your cord already cannot be broken, so imagine how much more once you start to weave new life on it. Each strand you weave into it makes it stronger and stronger. Does this mean that you're doomed to have to live with the cord you have weaved? Yes. But it's not a DOOM. It's a gift. You have become an addict. A person who does a thing over and over and will make sure that it happens no matter what. Whether that habit is good or bad, it's completely up to you.

FINAL THOUGHT

Revelation 12:10–11: "...Now salvation, and strength, and the kingdom of our God, and the power of His Christ have come, for the accuser of our brethren, who accused them before God day and night, has been cast down. And they overcame him by the blood of the Lamb and by the word of their testimony..."

Before we begin the final leg of this journey, please go back and read that last verse one more time...

We have an accuser; his name is Satan. In fact, the word Satan literally means accuser. And he's up there, in Heaven, accusing us, to God Himself. And the worst part is, everything he says is true. We have lied, we have cheated, and we have stolen. We do hold envy and strife in our hearts. And the list goes on.

But what does the verse go on to say? We overcome the accuser.

You ever been on trial, or gone in front of the judge for a crime that you actually did commit? Imagine if there was someone there at your hearing to say, "Your Honor, I accept responsibility for this one." No matter the charge, you go free.

That's the blood of the Lamb. That's the first step in overcoming the accuser, allowing Jesus to represent us. If we deny his council, we're left to defend ourselves. And all of the evidence is stacked against us, the punishment is going to be the max. Who wouldn't accept the free pardon?

In fact the Bible gives us a very clear example of what this exchange looks like:

Zechariah 3:1–4: "Then he showed me Joshua the high priest standing before the Angel of the LORD, and Satan standing at his right hand to oppose him. And the LORD said to Satan, 'The LORD rebuke you, Satan! The LORD who has chosen Jerusalem rebuke you! Is this not a brand plucked from the fire?' Now Joshua was clothed with filthy garments, and standing before the Angel. Then He answered and spoke to those who stood before Him, saying, 'Take away the filthy garments from him.' And to him He said, 'See I have removed your iniquity from you, and I will clothe you with rich robes.'"

But here's where it gets hairy, here's where you have a responsibility to respond to the free gift of salvation. Look back to the first verse from Revelation, "And by the word of their testimony." That's the second part to overcoming the accuser. You have to tell others about what happened.

"Everything done in the dark will come to the light." Take those things you did while operating in the realm of darkness and shed light on them. Speak about the goodness of God and what He's done for you. Remove the power that the enemy has and do it by speaking the word of your testimony. It's yours, and no one on this earth has a testimony quite like it.

I thank you for allowing me to share my testimony with you. God bless and may all of your days be saturated in the goodness of God.